I0867305

Nina's Favorite

MITTENS & SOCKS FROM AROUND NORWAY

Over 40 Traditional Knitting Patterns Inspired by Norwegian Folk-Art Collections

NINA GRANLUND SÆTHER

TRAFALGAR SQUARE
North Pomfret, Vermont

First published in the United States of America
in 2023 by
Trafalgar Square Books
North Pomfret, Vermont

Originally published in Norwegian as *Ninas beste votter og sokker*.

Copyright © 2021 Nina Granlund Sæther and Cappelen Damm AS
English translation © 2023 Trafalgar Square Books

All rights reserved. No part of this book may be reproduced, by any means, without written permission of the publisher, except by a reviewer quoting brief excerpts for a review in a magazine, newspaper or website.

The instructions and material lists in this book were carefully reviewed by the author and editor; however, accuracy cannot be guaranteed. The author and publisher cannot be held liable for errors.

ISBN: 978-1-64601-164-3
Library of Congress Control Number: 2022948770

Cover design: RM Didier
Interior design and layout: Sissel Holt Boniface
Photography: Guri Pfeifer, except for p. 11 courtesy of Nina Granlund Sæther
Charts: Nina Granlund Sæther
Translation into English: Carol Huebscher Rhoades

Printed in China
10 9 8 7 6 5 4 3 2 1

Table of Contents

Clothes to Stay Warm

Here in Norway, it's always been necessary to make garments to protect ourselves when the cold bites; that's why we have such long-standing traditions for making mittens and socks out of wool. In the seventeenth century, we also began to knit. The technique was easy to learn, the tools were simple and inexpensive, and the results were supple, comfortable-to-wear garments. The best known Norwegian knitting products are Selbu mittens and stockings, from the little village of the same name, east of Trøndelag—these were already knit for sale in the late nineteenth century. In the 1930s, the production volume was enormous. In 1937, more than 90,000 pairs of mittens were exported from Norway to the US, and to winter sports centers south of Norway in Europe. When Norwegian ski teams began wearing Selbu knitting at competitions, these clothes became high fashion for everyone, including here in Norway.

However, not everything knitted in two colors is from Selbu. Completely by chance, I came across a pair of old, pretty "rose mittens" from Skjåk. It occurred to me that they'd been constructed completely differently than Selbu mittens. Selbu mittens have different patterns on the back of the hand and the palm, and the top is always shaped in a point. The mittens from Skjåk had the same pattern all around, and the top was more rounded. That made me think—in the same way that folk and national costumes vary from place to place in Norway, we must also have had local mitten traditions. I wanted to research further, and I began to look into books on the Digital Museum.

In 2015, I was awarded a generous stipend from the Author's Fund. This grant made it possible for me to travel around Norway to hunt for old mittens. Over six months, I was able to visit more than twenty museums in ten of Norway's counties.

Unfortunately, textiles are perishable, and mittens quickly wear out. A darned and repaired mitten isn't as elegant as a new, whole one. Many mittens originally knitted for holidays and festive occasions were, over time, downgraded to everyday mittens. When they could no longer be repaired, they were thrown out or sent to a shoddy mill. The wool could then be re-carded and spun again. Therefore, the number of preserved traditional mittens isn't that large. Nevertheless, some remarkable treasures have survived the ravages of time. The mittens I found inspired me to make new patterns, and 43 pairs of mittens found a home in my book Mittens from Around Norway. Selbu mittens are extremely lovely, and considered almost a national symbol—but it was important to me to also shine a light on lesser-known patterns from Halden and Kristiansand in the south and Kautokeino in the north.

In 2017, I began to research again, and this time I was looking for old sock patterns. I found inspiration in well-worn knitted stockings from all over the country. More than 40 pairs were collected in my next book, Socks from Around Norway. Now, I've chosen the best mitten and sock patterns from these two books and collected them here. You'll also find several new patterns.

I often find myself excited and inspired by patterns from preserved garments, but I'm not compelled to make exact copies. The yarn is typically different, and I tend to play with more colors than were traditionally in use. I've also made some adjustments so the mittens and socks will be as easy to work and user-friendly as possible for modern knitters.

At a time when most people can buy anything they need and textiles are mainly produced in faraway low-wage countries, I hope others will experience happiness in the form of making their own garments. Yes, it takes time and can be very hard work, but you then get something completely different from typical mass-produced clothing. You get something that lasts longer, something you can relate to, something you can't be indifferent to. You'll have something that carries a unique and lasting cultural tradition further.

Nina Granlund Sæther

Nina Granlund Sæther på internett: www.hjertebank.no
Facebook: Hjertebank Nina Granlund Sæther
Instagram: @ninagranlundsather

Before You Begin: Tips and Techniques

NEEDLES

All the projects in this book are knitted with five double-pointed needles (dpn). Socks and stockings are worked from the cuff down, and mittens from the cuff up. Of course, you can work with a long magic loop circular instead; just remember the patterns are written with double-pointed needles in mind. The stitches are usually divided with the same number on each needle, but sometimes there will be more stitches on one side than on the other side.

The beginning and end of the round is at the side for mittens, and at the center back of the leg or centered on the sole for socks. The first needle holds the stitches for the left half of the back, the second needle has half of the left front; half of the right front stitches are on the third needle, and the fourth needle has the right half of the back.

I have divided the sock patterns into three sections: the leg, heel, and foot. The leg usually begins with ribbing or an edging, and the foot ends with the toe shaping.

ABBREVIATIONS

BO	bind off (= UK cast off)
CC	contrast (pattern) color
cm	centimeter(s)
CO	cast on
dec	decrease
dpn	double-pointed needles
dst	double stitch (for German short rows)
est	established = continue pattern as set
in	inch(es)
inc	increase
k	knit
k2tog or k3tog	knit 2 (3) together = 1 (2) stitches decreased; right-leaning decrease
m	meter(s)
M1	make 1 = increase one stitch by picking up the yarn between two stitches with the left needle tip, from the front, and knitting directly into the back loop
MC	main (background) color
mm	millimeter(s)
p	purl
p2tog	purl 2 stitches together = 1 stitch decreased
pm	place marker
psso	pass slipped st(s) over
rem	remain(s)(ing)
rnd(s)	round(s)
RS	right side
sl	slip
ssk	[slip 1 knitwise] 2 times, knit the 2 sts together through back loops = 1 stitch decreased; left-leaning decrease
st(s)	stitch(es)
St st	stockinette stitch (= UK stocking stitch)
tbl	through back loop(s)
WS	wrong side
wyb	with yarn held in back
wyf	with yarn held in front
yd	yard(s)
yo	yarnover

YARN AND REINFORCING THREAD

The patterns include yarn suggestions. Feel free to substitute yarn but adhere to the given gauge if you want the same results.

There are various yarn qualities suitable for socks. Sock yarns have a percentage of polyamide (nylon) or polyester for durability. These yarns are usually superwash-treated so the wool won't felt.

Norwegian Spelsau wool was the usual choice for sock yarn, historically. Spelsau fleece has both a soft undercoat and a strong, long outer coat. This combination makes the yarn especially durable. Today, many small mills market yarn from this wool.

Both horse and goat hair have been used to reinforce heels and soles on *ragg* socks (the word *ragg* refers to thick, shaggy goat hair). Women's hair was also used for reinforcement. Although we now prefer to use sock yarn strengthened with nylon, you might not want to use wool blended with other fibers. You can add in another strong thread instead, either for the whole sock or only for heels and perhaps the toes.

Finely-spun Spelsau yarn, such as Røros embroidery yarn, is a good choice for this, but the knitted fabric will be somewhat stiffer. You could also use silk thread or nylon buttonhole thread, which comes in a wide choice of colors (look for it in fabric shops). That adds less bulk and is barely visible.

For more information, see the section "Reinforcing the Heel" on page 20.

GAUGE

In order for finished garments to be the expected size, the suggested gauge must be maintained. If you knit too loosely, your garment will be too big. In that case, try smaller needles. And vice versa: if your knitting is too tight, your garment will be too small, so you should try bigger needles.

SIZING

Most of the mittens here are given in two sizes. The chart is the same for each size; sizing is adjusted by changing the gauge. If you want slightly longer mittens, work an additional 3–5 rounds before beginning the charted pattern.

Some of the socks in this book are written for one size only—women's shoe size U. S. 6½-9½ / Euro 37-40. If you want smaller socks, you can work with finer yarn and smaller needles; for larger socks, choose heavier yarn and bigger needles. You can also consult the table below for information about sizing.

In most cases, foot length can be adjusted. The toe shaping in these patterns measures 1¾-2¼ in / 4.5-6 cm long for adults and somewhat less for children's socks.

If your socks are a bit too large and you used pure, untreated wool yarn, you can lightly felt them to decrease the size slightly. Historically, it was common to felt socks to make them both warmer and more durable. For more information, see the section "Felting" on page 22.

Shoe Sizes U. S. / Euro	Foot Length	Approx. Size
6½-9½ / 37-40	9-9¾ in / 23-25 cm	Women's
8-11 / 41-44	10¼-11 in / 26-28 cm	Men's
12-15 / 45-48	11½-12¼ in / 29-31 cm	Men's XL

CASTING ON

There are many ways to cast on. For socks, the cast-on should be firm but not too tight. Choose a cast-on you like.

Some of the designs begin with a two-color cast-on. Begin with a slip knot of both colors held together and then continue with one strand of each color. One color forms the loops on the needle and the other the diagonals below (see drawing). When you begin knitting, remove the slip knot.

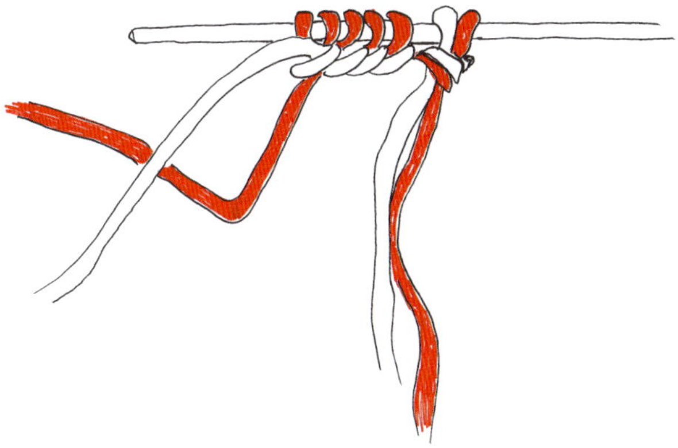

TWO-COLOR STRANDED KNITTING

When knitting patterns with two or more colors, it's important to make sure the strands aren't reversed on the wrong side. If you change the arrangement of the yarns at any point, it'll be very easy to see it on the right side.

YARN FLOATS

If you leave long floats on the inside of your knitting, it'll be all too easy to catch a finger or a toe on one. For patterns where the float is more than 5-6 stitches, I recommend you twist the strands around each other on the wrong side. Be careful not to stack these twists on top of each other; that will create a visible line of "blips" in the pattern on the right side.

PATTERN CHARTS

All the charts are read from right to left and from the bottom up. At the side of each chart, you'll find a key explaining the various symbols and colors. Where there are no squares, there are no stitches. If there's an open space in the chart, follow the line of the chart to the next square/stitch. When the number of stitches in the thumb gusset increases in width, you must add a stitch. Unless otherwise specified in the pattern with a dot where this should occur, increase a new stitch where shown in the drawing. When the number of stitches at the top decreases, it means you should decrease.

When knitting the left mitten, read the chart from left to right. If you find this challenging, you can always take a picture of the chart with your phone and then reverse it, and read the resulting mirror-imaged chart from right to left.

DECREASING

Right-leaning decrease: Slip 1 st, knit 1, pass slipped st over (or work ssk: slip 1 knitwise, slip 1 knitwise; insert left needle tip into sts left to right and knit the sts together).
Left-leaning decrease: Knit 2 sts together.

TWO-END (TWINED) KNITTING

In some patterns in this book, there are one or more rows of two-end knitting (also called twined knitting). The technique prevents the edge of a mitten or sock cuff from rolling up, so you don't need a traditional purled edging. This technique is both durable and decorative. It is worked with both yarns held in front of the work, winding them around each other in such a way as to form diagonal lines. It's most commonly done with two colors, but you can also work two-end knitting with two skeins of the same color. When you wind your yarns around each other in one direction on one round and in the opposite direction on the next, the result will look like a braid; this is called a Latvian braid in English.

A Latvian braid is worked in two colors—blue and white, for example:
Rnd 1: (K1 blue, k1 white) around.
Rnd 2: Bring both strands to the RS. Begin with blue and purl 1 over the previous blue stitch. Keeping the blue on the RS, move it to the right, laying it over the white strand. *Now bring the white strand under the blue, and purl 1 over the previous white stitch. Move the white to the right and over the blue strand. Bring the blue strand under the white, and purl 1. Always work blue over blue and white over white. Move the blue to the right and over the white.* Repeat these 2 stitches from * to * around. End with p1 white. Throughout, the strand you pick up always comes under the strand you just purled with.

As you work, the yarns will twist together. Just move the twist down and wait until the next round—once you're working in the opposite direction, the twist will disappear.

The second half of the braid is formed by reversing the twisting of the yarns.
Rnd 3: Begin with *purl 1 blue over the previous blue stitches. Keep the strand on the RS and to the right. Now bring the white yarn over the blue and purl 1. Move white to the right and beneath the blue on the RS*. Bring the blue over the white, and p1. Leave white

on RS to the right and down. Repeat these 2 stitches, from * to * around. End with p1 white. Throughout, the yarn to be used next comes over the previous strand. If you've worked this second purl round correctly, the yarns will have untwisted by the end of the round.

WEAVING IN YARN ENDS

It's important to weave in all ends well. Weave in on the wrong side by sewing through the ridges. Sew in one direction, turn, and sew back. Make sure the ends don't show on the right side.

Knitting Thumbs

Thumbs can be worked in several ways. In Norway, it's common to knit thumbs both with and without a gusset. A gusset is made by increasing a number of stitches from the ribbed cuff and up. The increases can be made on each side of the gusset, in the middle, or, less commonly, only on one side. In some places, it's also been common to knit the thumb separately and sew it on afterwards.

When the instructions say, "Set aside 15 sts for the thumb," it's easiest to knit those 15 sts with smooth scrap yarn in a contrast color. Slip the stitches back to the left needle and knit them with the working yarn (either single color or as shown on the chart).

When the rest of the mitten is finished, pick up the stitches below and above the scrap yarn using a double-pointed needle. (For example, the pattern might say, "pick up 17 + 17 sts for the thumb.") Use a double-pointed needle to pick up the stitches below the scrap yarn. To avoid holes, always begin 1 stitch to the right before the scrap yarn. Slide the needle from right to left, picking up the right leg of each stitch. Continue across until you have the specified number of stitches.

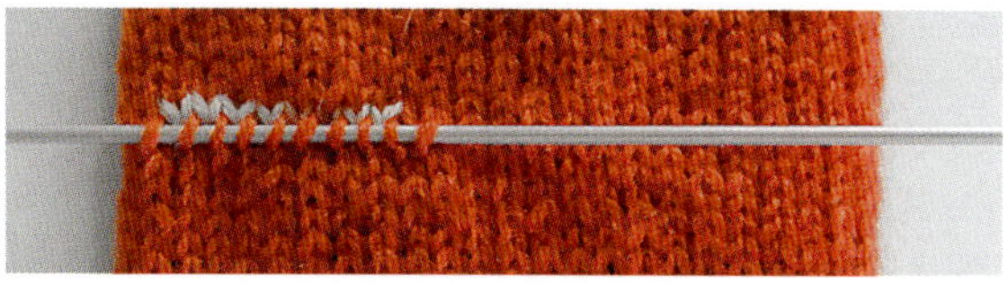

Turn the mitten upside down and follow the same procedure for the stitches above the scrap yarn. Begin 1 stitch to the right of the scrap yarn. Continue, picking up the right leg of each stitch until you have the specified number of stitches on the needle.

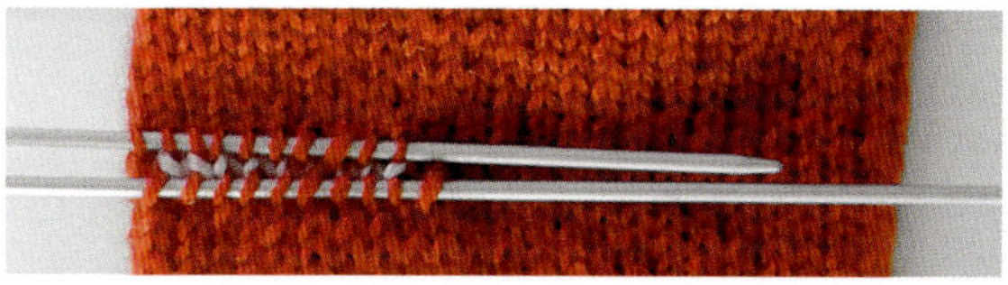

Carefully remove the scrap yarn and divide the stitches onto 4 needles.

In some of the patterns in this book, the stitch counts below and above the thumbhole don't match. In that case, don't use the scrap yarn method for setting aside stitches. Instead, slip the thumb stitches onto a safety pin, a length of yarn, or a yarn holder. On the next round, cast on the specified number of stitches.

Knitting Heels

Feet are different. Some people have narrow feet and others have wide ones. The height over the instep also varies. Heels can be formed in many ways and the heel type we prefer often depends on what fits our feet best. At one point, in Norway, it was standard to use what we now call the "common" heel, with a slight diagonal at the back of the heel and a sewn, or sometimes knitted, seam at the center of the base. I've also selected a few other heel options.

Knitting heels isn't difficult but can be a little challenging the first time. Ask someone who's knitted heels before for help or check the internet, where you'll find many good instructional videos.

When preparing to knit the heel, I recommend placing the instep stitches on a length of scrap yarn or a circular needle. This is because the stitches at each end will stretch less that way than if you leave them on two double-pointed needles. Using scrap yarn also helps avoid ugly holes or dropped stitches at the sides.

CHAIN STITCHES

When making the heel flap, slip stitches at each side to form a chain along the edge. Slip the first st of each row purlwise.

The chain forms as you work back and forth on two needles 1.

PICKING UP AND KNITTING STITCHES ALONG A HEEL FLAP

You have several options for picking up stitches along a heel flap. For example, you can pick up the chain sts and place them directly on the needle without knitting them. This is the easiest method. You can also knit the sts with the working yarn 2. You can pick up and knit through either one or both loops of the chain. Each way works just as well. Personally, I prefer to pick up and knit stitches through both loops.

You can pick up the stitches through back loops (twisted) or knit them through back loops on the next round 3.

1

2

3

HOURGLASS HEEL

This type of heel is worked back and forth with knit and purl stitches and shaped by working short rows. This means that the work is turned before the end of the row. Many people like this type of heel because it means you don't have to pick up stitches at the sides to work the foot.

How to Form the Hourglass Heel

After completing the leg, divide the stitches, placing instep stitches onto scrap yarn. These instep stitches will "rest" until the heel is complete.

Place the remaining stitches on one needle and work back and forth.

Row 1 (RS): Knit all the sts; turn.
Row 2: Sl 1, purl until 1 st rem; turn.
Row 3: Sl 1, knit until 1 st rem; turn.
Row 4: Sl 1, purl until 2 sts rem; turn.
Row 5: Sl 1, knit until 2 sts rem; turn.
Continue as est, with one st more rem at each side untl approx. ⅓ of the sts rem at the center of the heel (see table to right).
The last row is worked on RS.

Sl 1, purl as many sts as were knitted on the previous row. Pick up the strand between the last stitch and next stitch, twist it, and then purl it together with the next stitch; turn.

Sl 1, knit as many sts as were purled on the previous row. Pick up the strand between the last stitch and next stitch, twist it, and then knit it together with the next stitch; turn. Continue as est, repeating these 2 rows. Each row, you will have 1 more st before turning.

NOTE: Tighten the yarn a bit every time you turn to avoid holes.

Continue the same way with 1 more stitch on each row until the last row is worked over all the sts. Now work around on all stitches.

The following table can be used for socks shaped this way.

Total number of stitches	Stitches on instep	Stitches in center section of heel after decreasing
96	48	16
92	46	16
88	44	16
84	42	14
80	40	14
76	38	14
72	36	12
68	34	12
64	32	12
60	30	10
56	28	10
52	26	10
48	24	8
44	22	8
40	20	8
36	18	6
32	16	6
28	14	6
24	12	4
20	10	4

GUSSET HEEL

For a gusset heel, you first need to make a heel flap ending with a gusset at the base of the flap to follow the contour of your heel. The gusset's formed with short rows. Afterwards, pick up stitches along the sides of the heel flap and then decrease to eliminate the extra stitches at the same time as you begin the foot. The socks will then have a characteristic gusset at each side. This type of heel is particularly good if you have a high instep.

How to Form the Gusset Heel

After completing the leg, divide the stitches and place the instep stitches onto scrap yarn. These instep stitches will "rest" until the heel is complete.

Place the remaining stitches onto one needle and work back and forth. Begin with the WS facing you.
Row 1 (WS): Sl 1, purl to end of needle.
Row 2: Sl 1, knit to end of needle.
Repeat these 2 rows until the number of chains at each side of the flap is the same as half the stitch count on the needle (see table on next page).

Shaping the Heel

Row 1: Sl 1, purl until approx. ⅓ of the sts rem on the needle (see table—left side), p2tog, p1; turn.
Row 2: Sl 1, knit until approx. ⅓ of the sts rem on needle (see table—right side), ssk, k1; turn.
Row 3: Sl 1, purl until 1 st before gap, p2tog, p1; turn.
Row 4: Sl 1, knit until 1 st rem before gap, ssk, k1; turn.
Repeat Rows 3–4 until all the side sts have been eliminated.

Gusset Shaping

Divide the instep sts from the holder onto 2 dpn; divide the sole sts onto 2 dpn with half of the sts on each. With RS facing, begin working in the round. Begin rnd at center of sole. With Ndl 1, knit to flap; pick up and knit 1 st in each chain up side of flap. You can pick up the chain sts through back loops, or knit them through back loops on the next rnd. Work across the instep (the sts which had been "resting") with Ndls 2 and 3. Next, with Ndl 4, pick up and knit sts down opposite side of flap as for the first side. Knit to center of sole.

On the next rnd, begin decreasing to shape the gusset: Knit until 2 sts rem on Ndl 1, k2tog. Work across instep sts on Ndls 2-3. On Ndl 4, ssk and then knit to end of rnd.
Work the next rnd without decreasing.

Repeat these 2 rnds until you have the same number of sts as for the leg. Continue knitting the foot without decreasing.

Total number of stitches	Stitches on heel flap	Chain stitches at each side of heel flap	Heel flap left side	Heel flap center	Heel flap right side
96	48	24	16	16	16
92	46	23	15	16	15
88	44	22	15	14	15
84	42	21	14	14	14
80	40	20	13	14	13
76	38	19	13	12	13
72	36	18	12	12	12
68	34	17	11	12	11
64	32	16	11	10	11
60	30	15	10	10	10
56	28	14	9	10	9
52	26	13	9	8	9
48	24	12	8	8	8
44	22	11	7	8	7
40	20	10	7	6	7
36	18	9	6	6	6
32	16	8	5	6	5
28	14	7	5	4	5
24	12	6	4	4	4
20	10	5	3	4	3

This chart can be used for socks shaped as for the Gusset Heel and on Band Heels with a long heel flap.

BAND HEEL WITH SHORT HEEL FLAP

Band heels can be made with either a short or long heel flap. Short flaps work best for people with low arches. As for a gusset heel, you first need to make a heel flap, ending with a gusset at the base of the flap to follow the contour of your heel. The gusset is formed with short rows. Afterwards, pick up stitches along the sides of the heel flap and then decrease to eliminate the extra stitches at the same time as you begin the foot.

How to Form the Band Heel

After completing the leg, divide the stitches and place the instep stitches onto scrap yarn. These instep stitches will "rest" until the heel is complete.

Heel Flap

Place the remaining stitches onto one needle and work back and forth. Begin with the WS facing you.

Row 1 (WS): Sl 1, purl to end of needle.

Row 2: Sl 1, knit to end of needle.

Repeat these 2 rows until the number of chains at each side of the flap is the same as the appropriate count given in the table on the next page.

Shaping the Heel

Row 1: Sl 1, purl until approx. ⅓ sts rem on the needle (see table—left side), p2tog; turn.

Row 2: Sl 1, knit until approx. ⅓ of the sts rem on needle (see table—right side), ssk; turn.

Row 3: Sl 1, purl until 1 st before gap, p2tog; turn.

Row 4: Sl 1, knit until 1 st before gap, ssk; turn.

Repeat Rows 3–4 until all the side sts have been eliminated.

Gusset Shaping

Divide the instep sts from the holder onto 2 dpn; divide the sole sts onto 2 dpn with half of the sts on each. With RS facing, begin working in the round. Begin rnd at center of sole. With Ndl 1, knit to flap; pick up and knit 1 st in each chain up side of flap. You can pick up the chain sts through back loops, or knit them through back loops on the next rnd. Work across the instep (the sts which had been "resting") with Ndls 2 and 3. Next, with Ndl 4, pick up and knit sts down opposite side of flap as for the first side. Knit to center of sole.

Total number of stitches	Stitches on heel flap	Chain stitches at each side of heel flap	Heel flap left side	Heel flap center	Heel flap right side
96	48	16	17	14	17
92	46	15	16	14	16
88	44	15	16	12	16
84	42	14	15	12	15
80	40	13	14	12	14
76	38	13	14	10	14
72	36	12	13	10	13
68	34	11	12	10	12
64	32	11	12	8	12
60	30	10	11	8	11
56	28	9	10	8	10
52	26	9	10	6	10
48	24	8	9	6	9
44	22	7	8	6	8
40	20	7	8	4	8
36	18	6	7	4	7
32	16	5	6	4	6
28	14	5	6	2	6
24	12	4	5	2	5

This chart can be used for socks shaped as for the Band Heel with a short heel flap.

BAND HEEL WITH LONG HEEL FLAP

Band heels with long flaps work well for those with either a high or low arch. The gusset is formed as for a band heel with a short heel flap, except the flap is worked until the number of chain stitches at each side equals half the number of stitches on the needle. Begin with a heel flap ending with a gusset at the base of the flap to follow the contour of your heel. It's formed with short rows. Afterwards, pick up stitches along the sides of the heel flap and then decrease to eliminate the extra stitches at the same time as you begin the foot. You can work the shaping one of two ways: either by making a gusset at each side as for a regular gusset heel or by centering the decreases on the sole.

How to Form the Band Heel

After completing the leg, divide the stitches and place the instep stitches onto scrap yarn. These instep stitches will "rest" until the heel is complete.

Place the remaining stitches onto one needle and work back and forth. Begin with the WS facing you.
Row 1 (WS): Sl 1, purl to end of needle.
Row 2: Sl 1, knit to end of needle.
Repeat these 2 rows until the number of chains at each side of the flap equals half the number of stitches in the heel flap. Use the same table as for the gusset heel on page 15.

Shaping the Heel

Now shape the band:
Row 1: Sl 1, purl until approx. ⅓ sts rem on the needle (see table—left side), p2tog; turn.
Row 2: Sl 1, knit until approx. ⅓ of the sts rem on needle (see table—right side), ssk; turn.
Row 3: Sl 1, purl until 1 st before gap, p2tog; turn.
Row 4: Sl 1, knit until 1 st rem before gap, ssk; turn.
Repeat Rows 3-4 until all the side sts have been eliminated.

Divide the instep sts from the holder onto 2 dpn; divide the sole sts onto 2 dpn with half of the sts on each. With RS facing, begin working in the round. Begin rnd at center of sole. With Ndl 1, knit to flap; pick up and knit 1 st in each chain up side of flap. You can pick up the chain sts through back loops, or knit them through back loops on the next rnd. Work across the instep (the sts which had been "resting") with Ndls 2 and 3. Next, with Ndl 4, pick up and knit sts down opposite side of flap as for the first side. Knit to center of sole.

See photo on page 12.

Gusset Shaping at the Sides

Knit until 2 sts remain on Ndl 1, k2tog. Work across Ndls 2-3. On Ndl 4, ssk, and knit to end of rnd. Do not decrease on the next rnd. Repeat these 2 rnds until you have the same number sts as for the leg. Continue knitting foot without decreasing.

Shaping on the Sole

Knit until 2 sts rem at the lower edge on the left side of the heel gusset, k2tog. Knit to end of needle. Work around to beginning of heel gusset, ssk before knitting the rest of the sts on the needle. Do not decrease on the next rnd. Repeat these 2 rnds until all the stitches on the bottom of the heel flap have been eliminated and you have the same number sts as for the leg. Continue knitting foot without decreasing.

SHAPED COMMON HEEL

A gusset heel begins with a heel flap, shaped by a small gusset to follow the contour of a heel. This is made by decreasing some of the stitches and joining the rest at the center of the sole. Afterwards, stitches are picked up and knitted along each side of the heel flap. No extra stitches remain that need to be eliminated around the heel.

How to Form the Shaped Common Heel

After completing the flap, divide the stitches, placing the instep stitches on scrap yarn. These instep stitches will "rest" until the heel is complete. Common heels often have more stitches on the heel flap than on the instep—see chart.

Heel Flap

Divide the remaining stitches onto two dpn (Ndls A and B) and work back and forth. Begin with the RS facing you.

Row 1: Sl 1, knit rem sts on Ndls A and B.

Row 2: Sl 1, purl rem sts on Ndls A and B.

Repeat these 2 rows until the number of chains at each side of the flap matches the number given in the chart.

Shaping the Heel

Now you will shape the back by decreasing as follows:

Row 1: Sl 1, knit until 5 sts rem on Ndl A, k2tog, k3. On Ndl B, k3, ssk, knit to end of needle.

Row 2: Sl 1, purl to end of row.

Row 3: Sl 1, knit until 4 sts rem on Ndl A, k2tog, k2. On Ndl B, k2, ssk, knit to end of needle.

Row 4: Sl 1, purl to end of row.

Row 5: Sl 1, knit until 3 sts rem on Ndl A, k2tog, k1. On Ndl B, k1, ssk, knit to end of needle.

Row 6: Sl 1, purl to end of row.

Row 7: Sl 1, knit until 2 sts rem on Ndl A, k2tog. On Ndl B, ssk, knit to end of needle.

Row 8: Sl 1, purl to end of first needle. Yarn is now at center of heel flap.

Hold the two dpn with RS facing (so WS faces out on each side). Join the sets of sts with 3-needle BO: K2tog with 1 st from each needle, *k2tog with next st from each needle, pass first st over the second*. Repeat from * to * until 1 st loop rem.

Divide the instep sts onto 2 dpn. With RS facing and Ndl 1, beginning at the center of the sole, pick up and knit 1 st in each chain st on the side of the flap. You can pick up the chain sts through back loops or knit them tbl on the next rnd. Work the instep sts on Ndls 2–3 (those that had been "resting"). With Ndl 4, pick up and knit sts on the opposite side of the heel flap.

Total number of stitches	Stitches on instep	Stitches on heel flap	Chain stitches on each side of flap before decreasing
96	40	56	24
92	38	54	23
88	36	52	22
84	34	50	21
80	34	46	19
76	32	44	18
72	30	42	17
68	28	40	16
64	26	38	15
60	24	36	14
56	22	34	13
52	22	30	11
48	20	28	10
44	18	26	9
40	16	24	8
36	14	22	7
32	12	20	6

REINFORCING THE HEEL

The heel is the part of a sock that's the most likely to wear out. There are several techniques for reinforcing heels so they'll be stronger and more durable. You can knit with two colors, with reinforcing thread, doubled yarn, or knit a reinforced heel.

Reinforced Heel

Begin with WS facing you.

Row 1: Sl 1, purl to end of row.

Row 2: Sl 1, *k1, sl 1*; rep * to * to last st and end k1.

Repeat these 2 rows until you have the required number of chain sts on each side of the heel flap. You can continue repeating these two rows for the gusset under the flap, or you can work it in stockinette.

Sewing in Reinforcing Thread

Another method for reinforcing the heel after the heel has been worked is to sew in reinforcing thread through the ridges on the wrong side, threading it in as if weaving in ends.

TOE SHAPING

There are a number of ways to shape toes; I've described two of the most common methods here. The length of the toe is between 1¼ and 2½ in / 4.5 and 6 cm for adult sizes and somewhat less for children.

Star Toe

Begin the round at the center of the sole.
Rnd 1: (K5, k2tog) around.
Rnds 2-6: Knit.
Rnd 7: (K4, k2tog) around.
Rnds 8-11: Knit.
Rnd 12: (K3, k2tog) around.
Rnds 13-15: Knit
Rnd 16: (K2, k2tog) around.
Rnds 17-18: Knit.
Rnd 19: (K1, k2tog) around.
Rnd 20: Knit.
Rnd 21: (K2tog) around.

Cut yarn and draw end through rem sts; tighten. If the beginning number of sts is not a multiple of 7, there will be one or more stitches left on the last needle of the first rnd. These extra stitches will be decreased on subsequent rounds.

Wedge Toe

Divide the sts with the same number on each of the 4 dpn. Begin at the center of the sole.
Rnd 1:
Ndl 1: Knit until 3 sts rem on needle, k2tog, k1.
Ndl 2: K1, ssk, knit to end of needle.
Ndl 3: Work as for Ndl 1.
Ndl 4: Work as for Ndl 2.
Rnd 2: Knit without decreasing.

Repeat these two rounds 4 times and then decrease on every rnd until approx. 6 sts rem on each needle.

Slip the sts from Ndl 1 onto Ndl 4 and from Ndl 3 to Ndl 2 so there are 12 sts on each of the two needles. Turn the work inside out so the WS faces out. Holding the two needles together, push them out so you can work the 3-needle BO. If it's difficult to move the needles through the hole at the tip of the toe, you can move the sts onto scrap yarn before you turn the sock inside out and then place them back on the needles once the stitches are in place.

Join the sets of stitches with 3-needle BO:
K2tog with 1 st from each needle, *k2tog with next st from each needle, pass first st over the second*. Repeat from * to * until all sts have been joined. Cut yarn and draw end through rem st. Fasten off well.

GARMENT CARE AND FELTING

To ensure your mittens and socks are professionally finished, wash them in lukewarm water with a mild, wool-safe soap, block them, and dry them on mitten or sock blockers, if you have them. They can also be dried flat. If your items have edgings—lace, for example (as for the Block Socks on page 75)—the lace should be pinned out to dry so it will be smooth. Spray with lukewarm water if the pieces have dried out, and leave them pinned until they are completely dry (at least 24 hours).

If your mittens or socks are a bit too big, they can be lightly felted by hand. That will make them warmer and more durable, but a little less elastic. Felting works best with pure non-superwash wool.

Use a felting board or washboard, a tub with lukewarm water and soap—for example, Milo, Zalo, or Green soap. If you want your pieces to be shorter, lay them out diagonally, and rub back and forth. Continue to rub until the mittens or socks are the right size. Rinse out the soap, shape the items, and lay them flat. I recommend drying them on mitten or sock blockers.

Patterns

Sugar Top Mittens

Lofty wavy tops with a nice, gentle, sweet flavor—or, pure and simple, a pair of mittens as sweet as sugar.

INSTRUCTIONS
Sizes: Women's

MATERIALS
Yarn:
CYCA #1 (fingering) Finullgarn from Rauma (100% wool, 191 yd/175 m / 50 g):
Black 410: 50 g
Red 435: 50 g
Pink 4686: 50 g
Orange 4305: 50 g
Needles: U.S. size 1.5 / 2.5 mm, set of 5 dpn
Gauge: 30 sts = 4 in / 10 cm.
Adjust needle size to obtain correct gauge if necessary.

RIGHT MITTEN
With Black, CO 60 sts. Divide sts onto 4 dpn and join, being careful not to twist cast-on row. Knit 1 rnd.
Pattern Rnd 1: *K2tog, k2, yo, k1, yo, k2, k2tog tbl, p1*; rep * to * around.
Change to Red.
Pattern Rnd 2: *K9, p1*; rep * to * around.
Rep these 2 rnds 6 times total.
Change to Pink and work Pattern Rnds 1 and 2.
Change to Red and work Pattern Rnds 1 and 2.
Change to Pink and work Pattern Rnds 1 and 2.
Change to Red and work Pattern Rnds 1 and 2.
Change to Pink and work Pattern Rnds 1 and 2.
Change to Orange and work Pattern Rnds 1 and 2.
Change to Pink and work Pattern Rnds 1 and 2.
Change to Orange and work Pattern Rnds 1 and 2.
Change to Pink and work Pattern Rnds 1 and 2.
Purl 1 rnd.
Next 2 Rnds: *K2 Pink, k2 Black*; rep * to * around.

With Pink, knit 1 rnd and then purl 1 rnd. Change to Red and knit around, decreasing 6 sts evenly spaced around = 54 sts rem. Continue, following chart.

Shape thumb gusset as shown on chart. At dark line, place 14 thumb sts on a holder and CO 12 new sts over gap. Continue following chart, shaping top as shown.

THUMB
Pick up 15 + 15 sts = total of 30 sts (see page 15). Divide sts onto 4 dpn and work as shown on thumb chart. Cut yarn and draw end through rem sts; tighten.

LEFT MITTEN
Work as for right mitten, reversing thumb placement.

FINISHING
Weave in all ends neatly on WS. Gently steam press under a damp pressing cloth to block.

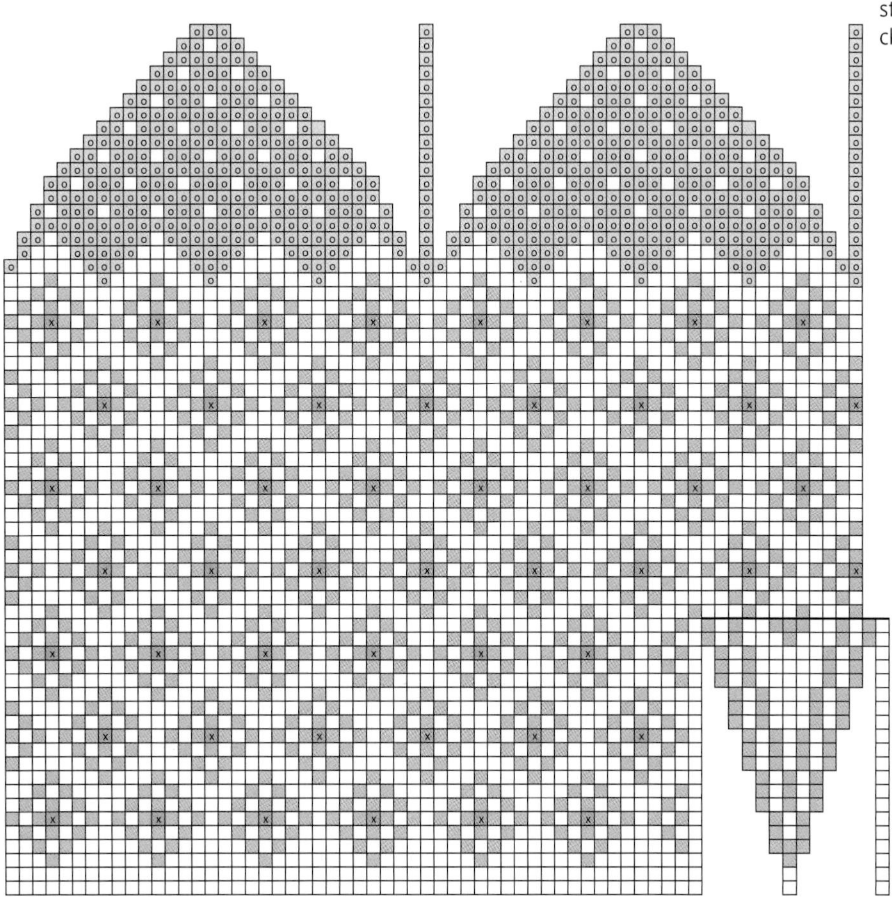

Thumb

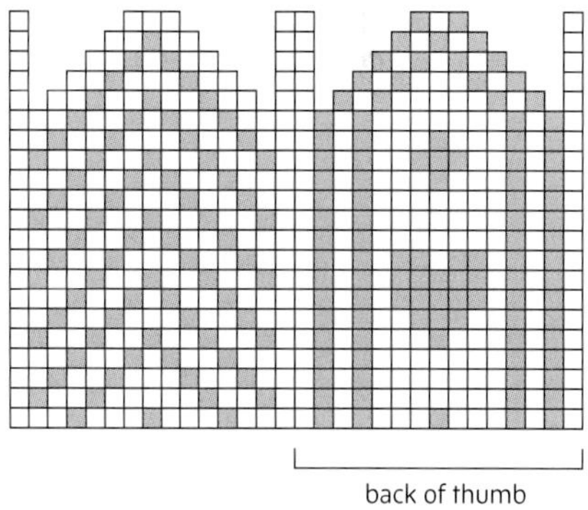

☐ Red
☐ Black
☐ Pink
☐ Pink and Orange held together

Thumb

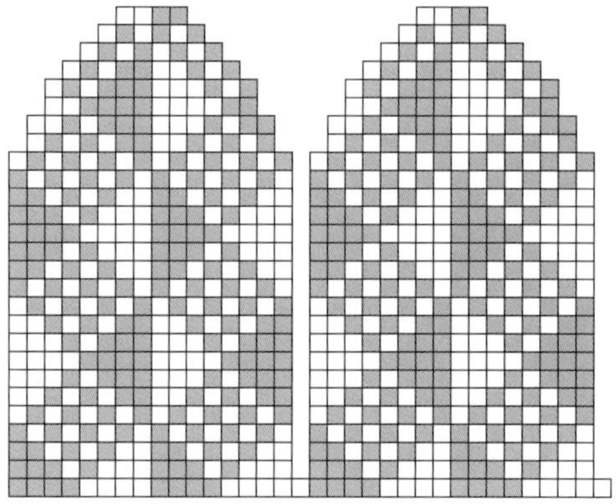

■ Gray—knit
□ Green—knit

← Set aside 16 sts for the thumb.

Mittens from Idd

A pair of mittens from the neighborhood of Ør in Idd—now Halden—has the date of 1858 knitted in on one cuff, and they are the oldest patterned mittens from Norway we can date with certainty. They have a simple block pattern in black and green repeated around the mitten. I knitted this pair with the same pattern motif as the 1858 originals, but decided to make the folded cuff a little longer, and omitted the date and initials.

INSTRUCTIONS
Sizes: Women's (Men's)

MATERIALS
Yarn:
CYCA #1 (fingering) 2-ply Gammelserie from Rauma (100% wool, 175 yd/160 m / 50 g), Gray 405: 50 (100) g
Løyegarn (embroidery yarn) from Setesdal Handcraft, Green 50 (100) g
OR substitute Dale Baby Ull [CYCA #1 (fingering), 100% wool (180 yd/165 m / 50 g)], Light Olive 2231
Needles: U.S. size 0 (1.5) / 2 (2.5) mm, set of 5 dpn
Gauge: 36 (33) sts = 4 in / 10 cm. Adjust needle size to obtain correct gauge if necessary.

RIGHT MITTEN
With Gray, CO 81 sts. Divide sts onto 4 dpn and join, being careful not to twist cast-on row. Work around in k2, p2 ribbing for 3½ in / 9 cm. Dec 1 st to 80 sts and continue in St st following the chart. At the dark line, set aside 16 sts for thumb (see page 15 for details). Shape top of mitten as shown on the chart (see page 13 for details). Cut yarn and draw end through rem sts; tighten.

THUMB
Pick up 17 + 17 sts = total of 34 sts (see page 15). Divide sts onto 4 dpn and work as shown on thumb chart. Cut yarn and draw end through rem sts; tighten.

LEFT MITTEN
Work as for right mitten, reversing thumb placement.

FINISHING
Weave in all ends neatly on WS. Gently steam press under a damp pressing cloth to block. Fold cuff up to double.

Oslo Socks

The Norwegian Museum of Cultural History has five white cotton children's stockings in its collection. The museum estimates they were knitted in the 1890s. Since there's only one stocking of each type and the stockings seem to have been numbered, I imagine these are stockings in a series made to help someone learn how to knit. As a starting point for my interpretation of the stockings, I took the stitch pattern from one of the stockings but made mine in fine wool yarn.

INSTRUCTIONS
Size: Women's

MATERIALS
Yarn: CYCA #1 (fingering) Baby Panda from Rauma Ullvarefabrikk (100% Merino wool, 191 yd/175 m / 50 g
Yarn Color and Amount:
White 11: 100
Needles: U. S. size 0 / 2 mm: set of 5 dpn
Gauge: 32 sts in pattern = 4 in / 10 cm.
Adjust needle size to obtain correct gauge if necessary.

LEG
CO 81 sts. Divide sts as evenly as possible onto 4 dpn. Join, being careful not to twist cast-on row. Pm for beginning of rnd—the pattern shifts to the right, so it's important to maintain the beginning of rnd marker. Knit 4 rnds. Turn work so WS faces you and continue, following the chart or the description below until piece measures approx. 4¾ in / 12 cm.

Pattern Repeat (multiple of 9 sts)
Rnd 1: *P1, yo, k6, k2tog*; rep * to * around.
Rnd 2: *P1, k1, yo, k5, k2tog*; rep * to * around.
Rnd 3: *P1, k2, yo, k4, k2tog*; rep * to * around.
Rnd 4: *P1, k3, yo, k3, k2tog*; rep * to * around.
Rnd 5: *P1, k4, yo, k2, k2tog*; rep * to * around.
Rnd 6: *P1, k5, yo, k1, k2tog*; rep * to * around.
Rnd 7: *P1, k6, yo, k2tog*; rep * to * around.

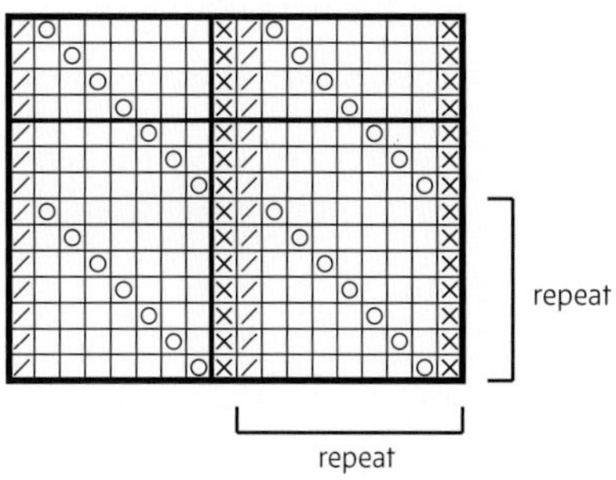

knit
purl
yarnover (yo)
k2tog

HEEL
After completing sock leg, place 41 sts on a holder for instep. These sts will "rest" until the heel is finished.

Heel Flap
Place the rem 40 sts on one dpn and work the heel flap back and forth. Begin with WS facing you.
Row 1 (WS): Sl 1 purlwise wyf, k2, p34, k3.
Row 2: Sl 1 purlwise wyb, knit across.
Rep these 2 rows until there are 20 chain sts at each side of flap.

Shaping Heel Gusset
Row 1: Sl 1, purl until 14 sts rem, p2tog, p1; turn.
Row 2: Sl 1, knit until 14 sts rem, ssk, k1; turn.
Row 3: Sl 1, purl until 1 st before gap, p2tog, p1; turn.
Row 4: Sl 1, knit until 1 st before gap, ssk, k1; turn.
Rep Rows 3-4 until all the side sts have been eliminated.

Gusset
Divide the instep sts onto 2 dpn and divide the rem heel sts onto 2 dpn so you have half of each section on a needle. Now work in the round with RS facing you. Begin rnd at center of heel. Knit to flap. Pick up and knit 1 st in each chain st along side of heel flap. You can pick up the sts tbl or knit them tbl on next rnd. Work across instep, rep (k2tog, k6) 4 times and ending with k2tog, and, *at the same time*, slip all yarnovers from last pattern rnd off needle (total of 5 sts) = 31 sts rem on instep. Pick up and knit 1 st in each chain st of opposite side of flap and knit to beginning of rnd at center of sole.

On the next rnd, begin shaping the gusset: Knit until 2 sts rem on Ndl 1, k2tog. Knit across Ndls 2-3. At beginning of Ndl 4, ssk and knit to end of rnd.
Knit 1 rnd without decreasing. Rep these 2 rnds until 64 sts rem. Continue in stockinette without decreasing until foot measures 7 in / 18 cm or desired length to toe shaping.

STAR TOE
Begin at the center of the sole.
Rnd 1: (K5, k2tog) around. The 1 st rem on Ndl 4 will be decreased in subsequent rnds.
Rnds 2-6: Knit.
Rnd 7: (K4, k2tog) around.
Rnds 8-11: Knit.
Rnd 12: (K3, k2tog) around.
Rnds 13-15: Knit
Rnd 16: (K2, k2tog) around.
Rnds 17-18: Knit.
Rnd 19: (K1, k2tog) around.
Rnd 20: Knit.
Rnd 21: (K2tog) around.

FINISHING
Cut yarn and draw end through rem sts; tighten. Weave in all ends neatly on WS. Make the second sock the same way.

FOOT

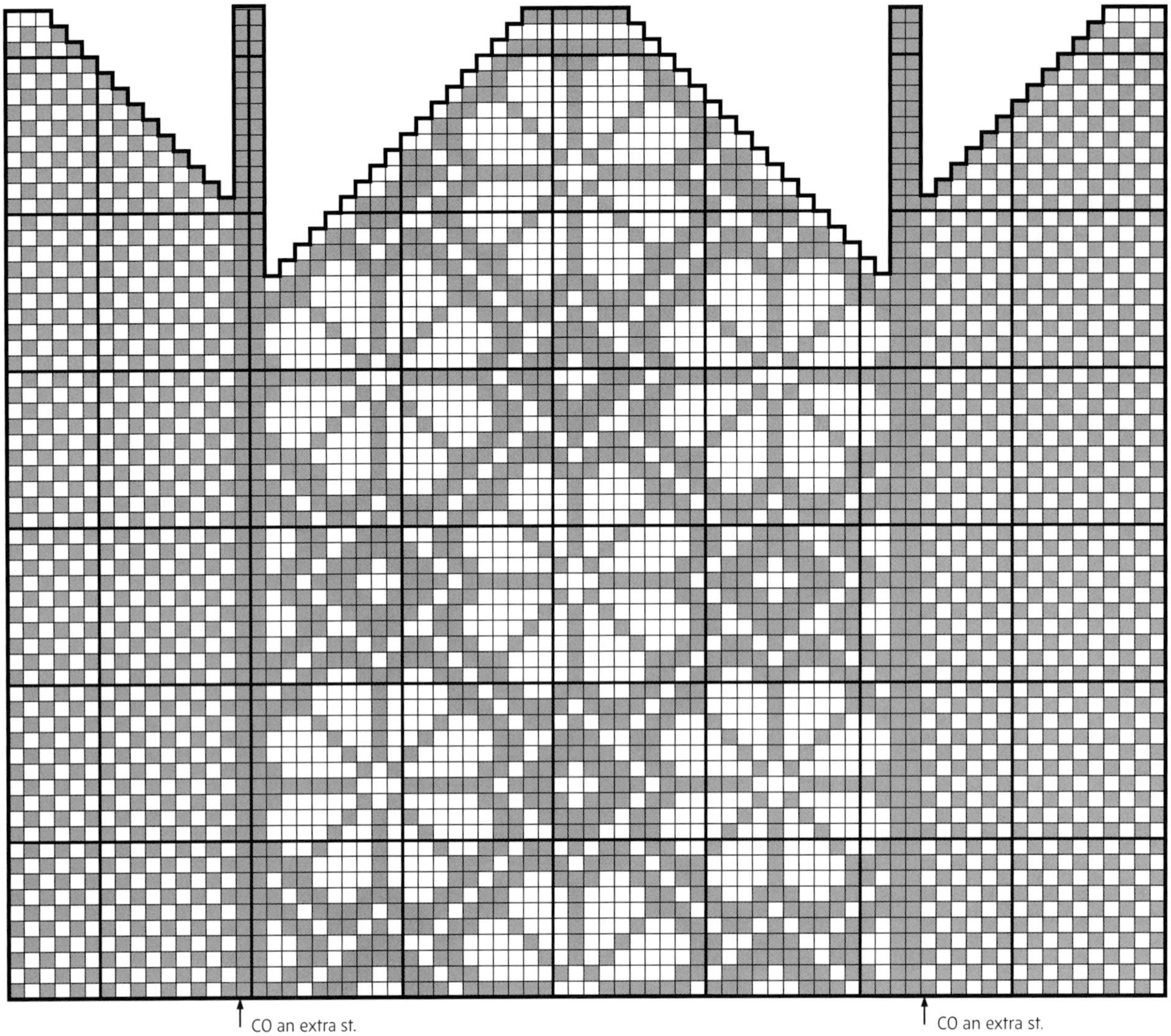

LEG

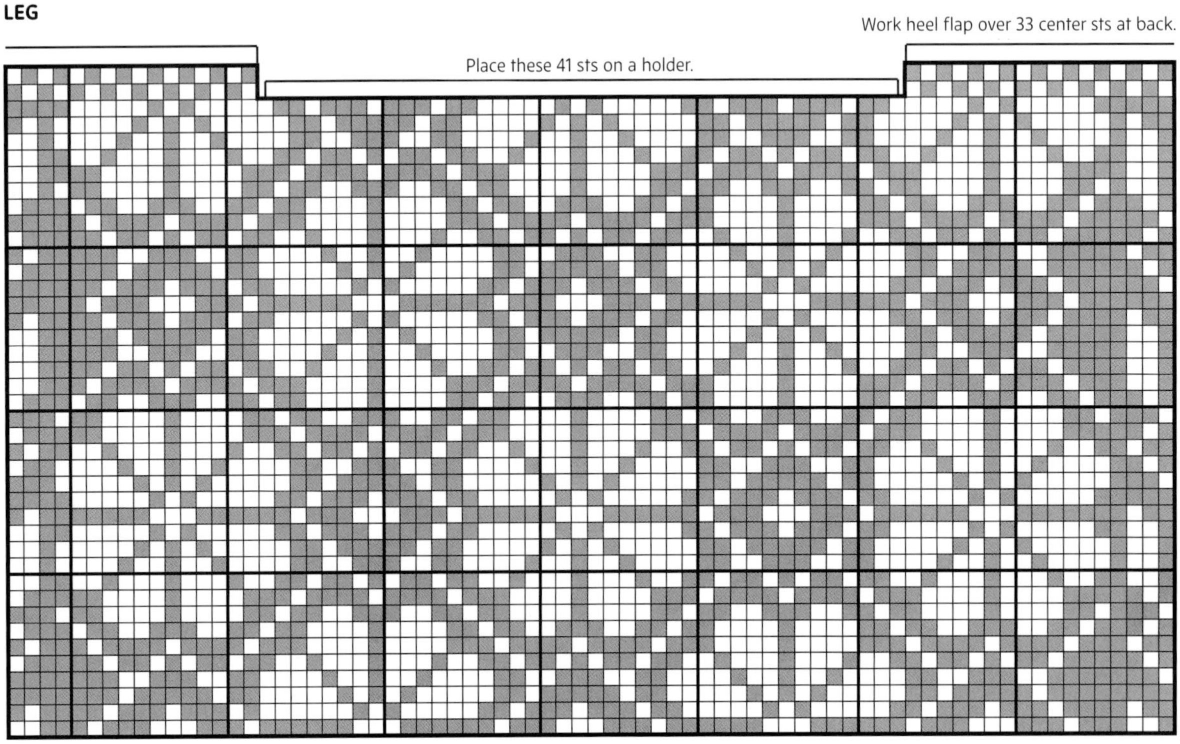

Charcoal Gray 807

Golden Yellow 835

Rose Stockings from Asker

In a bag of assorted woolens that were stored away, I found my father-in-law's old ski stockings. They were from a time when it was common to wear knickerbockers and patterned stockings for skiing, and they likely came from the period right after the war or the beginning of the 1950s. I'm reasonably sure the stockings were knitted by my husband's grandmother, Otilie Sæther, née Rønsen (1880-1964). She was originally from Eidsvoll and came to Asker in 1905 when the Dikemark hospital opened. Here, long stockings have become short socks.

INSTRUCTIONS
Sizes: Women's (Men's)

MATERIALS
Yarn: CYCA #1 (fingering) Mini Sterk from Du Store Alpakka (40% alpaca, 40% Merino wool, 20% polyamide, 182 yd/166 m / 50 g)
Yarn Colors and Amounts:
Charcoal Gray 807: 50 (100) g
Golden Yellow 835: 50 (100) g
Needles: U. S. size 1.5 (2.5) / 2.5 (3) mm: set of 5 dpn
Gauge: 34 (32) sts in pattern = 4 in / 10 cm.
Adjust needle size to obtain correct gauge if necessary.

LEG
With Golden Yellow, CO 72 sts. Divide sts evenly onto 4 dpn. Join, being careful not to twist cast-on row. Pm for beginning of rnd.
Work 8 rnds of k2, p2 ribbing. Knit 1 rnd, increasing 2 sts evenly spaced around = 74 sts. Now work following Leg chart.

After completing leg, place 41 sts on a holder for the instep (see chart). These sts will "rest" until the heel is finished.

BAND HEEL
Place the rem 33 sts on one dpn and work the heel flap back and forth with two colors as shown on the chart. Begin with WS facing you.
Row 1 (WS): Sl 1 purlwise wyf, purl to last st, end p1 with both colors.
Row 2: Sl 1 purlwise wyb, knit to last st, end k1 with both colors.
Rep these 2 rows until there are 12 chain sts at each side of flap.

Now decrease to shape the band:
Row 1: Sl 1, purl until 9 sts rem, p2tog with both colors; turn.
Row 2: Sl 1, knit until 9 sts rem, ssk with both colors; turn.
Row 3: Sl 1, purl until 1 st before gap, p2tog with both colors; turn.
Row 4: Sl 1, knit until 1 st before gap, ssk with both colors; turn.
Rep Rows 3-4 until all the side sts have been eliminated = 11 sts rem.

FOOT
Divide the instep sts onto 2 dpn and divide the rem heel sts onto 2 dpn so you have half of each section on a needle. Now work in the round with RS facing you. Begin rnd at center of heel. Work, alternating colors—see chart. Knit to flap. Pick up and knit 1 st in each chain st along side of heel flap. You can pick up the sts tbl or knit them tbl on next rnd. Work across instep following chart. Pick up and knit 1 st, alternating colors, in each chain st of opposite side of flap and then complete rnd as est = 76 sts total.

Work the foot following the chart.

TOE
Shape toe as shown on the chart. To decrease at right side: ssk with Golden Yellow. To decrease at left side: k2tog with Golden Yellow.

FINISHING
Cut yarn and draw end through rem sts; tighten. Weave in all ends neatly on WS. Make the second sock the same way.

FOOT

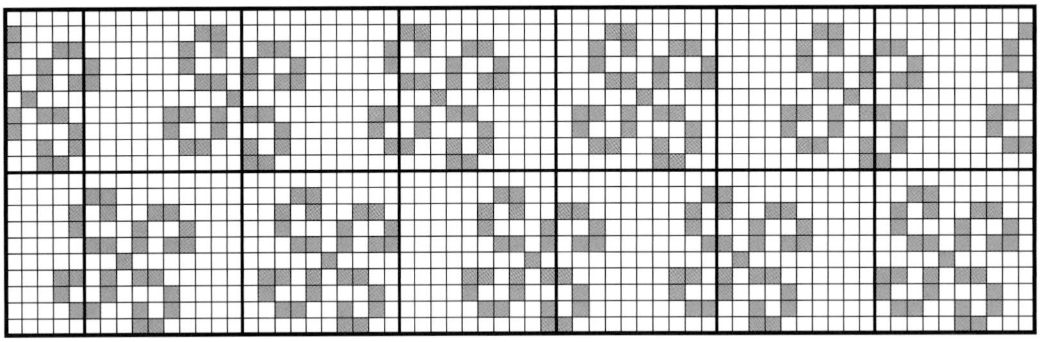

LEG

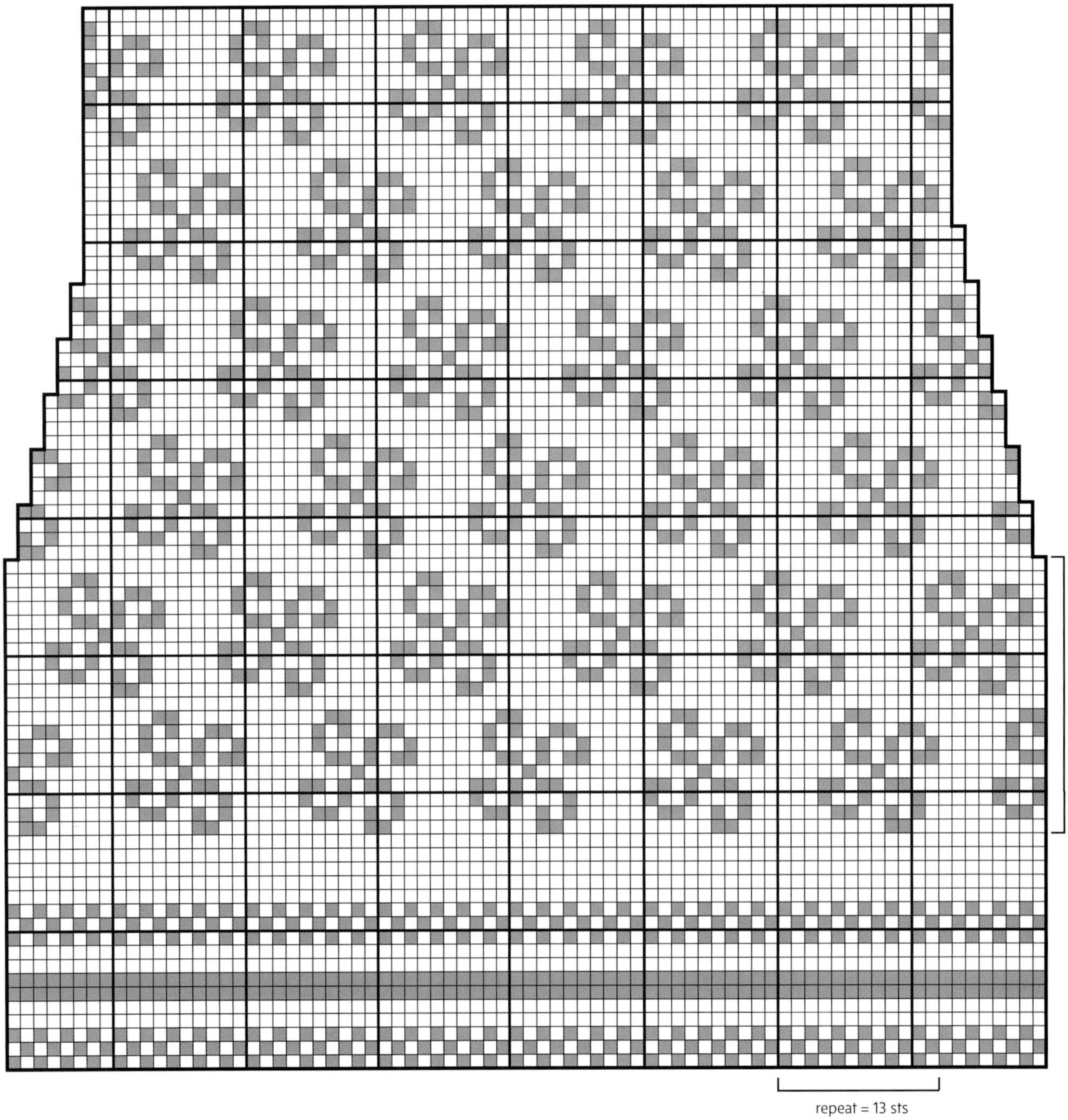

Stockings from 1868

In 1916, the Norwegian Museum of Cultural History acquired a pair of small children's stockings with red motifs on a white background. The records reveal only sparse details: "period of 1868-70." The stockings were knitted with very fine wool. Here, I've copied the pattern from those stockings in a thicker yarn, to make them the right size for an adult woman.

INSTRUCTIONS
Size: Women's

MATERIALS
Yarn:
CYCA #1 (fingering) 2-ply Gammelserie from Rauma (100% wool, 175 yd/160 m / 50 g): White 401, 100 g
CYCA #1 (fingering) Finullgarn from Rauma (100% wool, 191 yd/175 m / 50 g): Raspberry Red 456, 100 g
Needles:
U. S. size 1.5 / 2.5 mm: set of 5 dpn
Gauge: 28 sts in pattern = 4 in / 10 cm.
Adjust needle size to obtain correct gauge if necessary.

LEG
With Red, CO 78 sts. Divide sts as evenly as possible onto 4 dpn. Join, being careful not to twist cast-on row; pm for beginning of rnd. Knit 1 rnd.
Change to White and work in k3, p3 ribbing for 15 rnds.
Purl 1 rnd.
Next, work an eyelet rnd: (k2tog, yo) around.
Now work 15 rnds in stockinette and then work 1 repeat following chart. As shown on chart, decrease 2 sts at center back on every 4th rnd, but on the last rnd, decrease only 1 st = a total of 13 sts decreased and 65 sts rem.
Continue following the chart through last chart row = a total of 3 pattern repeats have been worked.

HOURGLASS HEEL
After completing sock leg, divide sts, placing 32 sts on a holder for instep. These sts will "rest" until the heel is finished.

Place rem 33 sts on one dpn and work back and forth with White.
Row 1 (RS): Sl 1 purlwise wyb, knit 32; turn.
Row 2: Sl 1 purlwise wyf, purl until 1 st rem; turn.
Row 3: Sl 1, knit until 1 st rem; turn.
Row 4: Sl 1, purl until 2 sts rem; turn.
Row 5: Sl 1, knit until 2 sts rem; turn.
Continue as est until 12 sts rem at center of heel. The last row is worked on RS.

Sl 1, work as many purl sts as last knitted (12 sts). Pick up the strand between the last st and next, twist it and purl it tog with the next st; turn.
Sl 1, knit as many sts as last worked (12 sts). Pick up strand between last st and next, twist it and knit it tog with next st; turn.
Rep these two rows, always with 1 more st before turning.
NOTE: Tighten the yarn a bit each time you turn to prevent holes.
Continue as est, with 1 st more on each row until, on the last row, you work all the sts across heel.

Now work in the round over all the sock sts. *At the same time*, work in pattern following the chart for the foot for 2 rep of charted rows. Cut Red and continue with White only.

STAR TOE
Begin at the center of the sole.
Rnd 1: (K5, k2tog) around. The 2 sts rem on Ndl 4 will be decreased in subsequent rnds.
Rnds 2-6: Knit.
Rnd 7: (K4, k2tog) around.
Rnds 8-11: Knit.
Rnd 12: (K3, k2tog) around.
Rnds 13-15: Knit
Rnd 16: (K2, k2tog) around.
Rnds 17-18: Knit.
Rnd 19: (K1, k2tog) around.
Rnd 20: Knit.
Rnd 21: (K2tog) around.

FINISHING
Cut yarn and draw end through rem sts; tighten. Weave in all ends neatly on WS. Make the second sock the same way.

- ☐ Natural 11
- ▩ Blue 83

FOOT

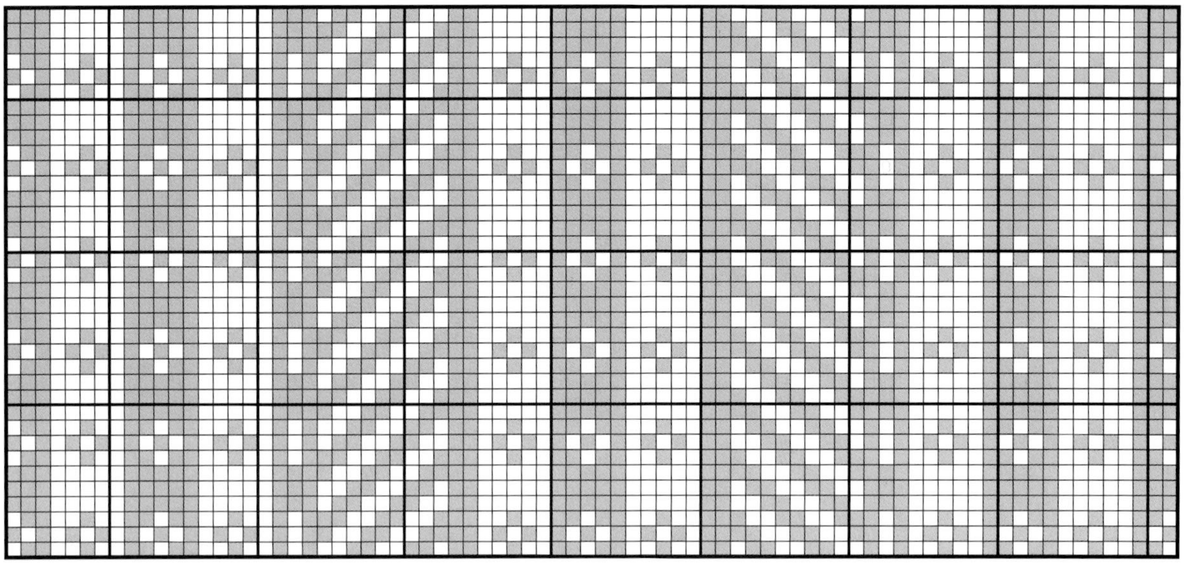

LEG

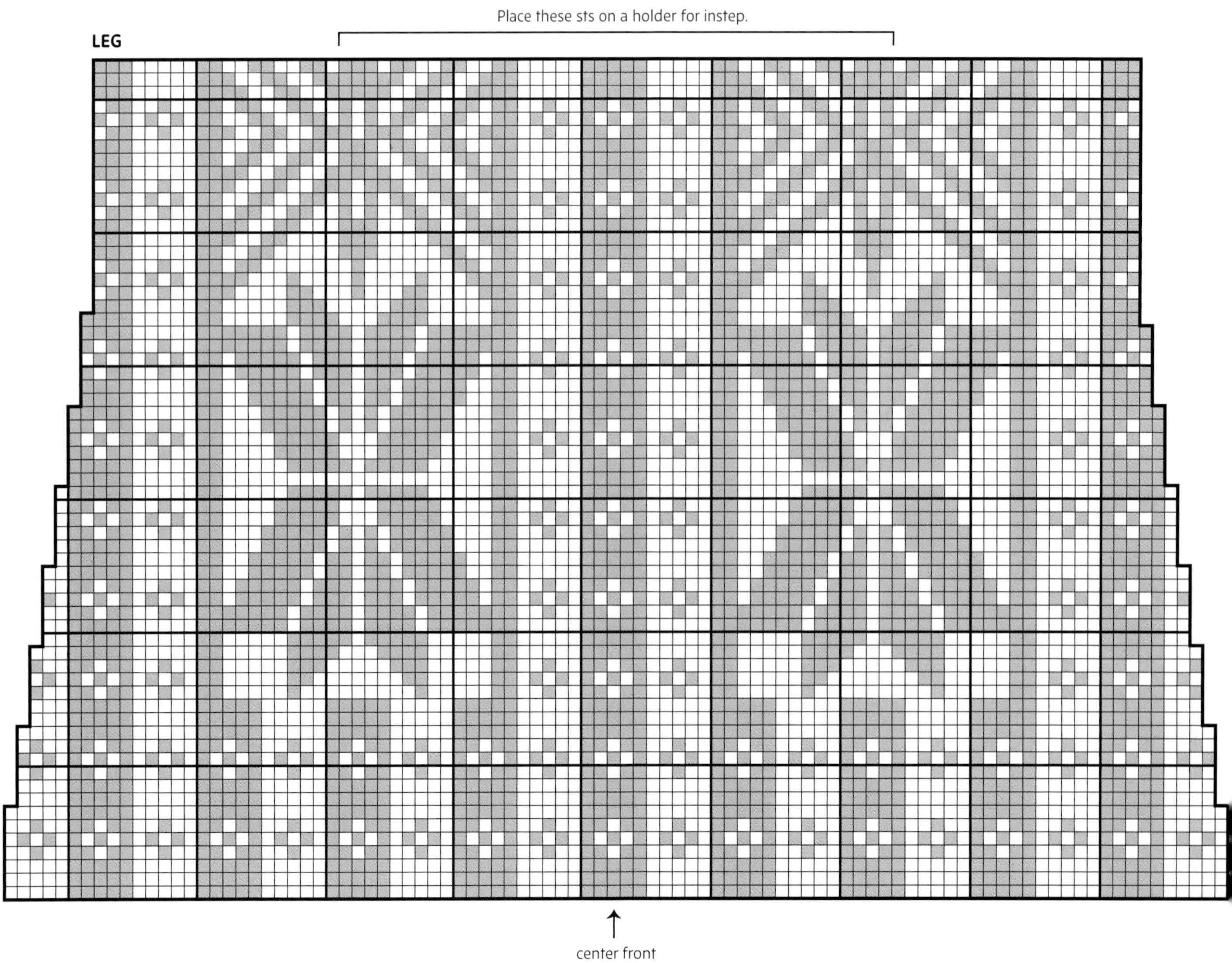

Rose Ankle Socks

The Norwegian Museum of Cultural History has a pair of long men's stockings with a simple stripe pattern and large, characteristic eight-petal roses at the ankles, usually called *okleroser* or "ankle roses" in Norwegian. Once people started knitting stockings, they copied elements from sewn stockings. So early knitted stockings—which were one color at the beginning—were made with a false "seam" of purl stitches at the center back of the leg and decorations at the ankles. Here's my shorter variation, with a pretty lace edging.

INSTRUCTIONS

Sizes: Women's (Men's)

MATERIALS

Yarn: CYCA #1 (fingering) Baby Panda from Rauma Ullvarefabrikk (100% Merino wool, 191 yd/175 m / 50 g)
Yarn Colors and Amounts:
Natural White 11: 100 (100) g
Blue 38: 100 (100) g
Needles: U. S. size 1.5 (2.5) / 2.5 (3) mm: set of 5 dpn
Gauge: 30 (28) sts in pattern = 4 in / 10 cm.
Adjust needle size to obtain correct gauge if necessary.

LEG

With Lace Edging

With Natural White, CO 96 sts. Divide sts evenly onto 4 dpn. Join, being careful not to twist cast-on row. Pm for beginning of rnd and work lace pattern as follows:
Rnd 1: *K2tog, k4, yo, k4, ssk*; rep * to * around.
Rnd 2: Knit.
Rnd 3: *K2tog, k3, yo, k1, yo, k3, ssk*; rep * to * around.
Rnd 4: K4, *ssk, k9*; rep * to * around, ending with ssk, k5.
Rnd 5: *K2tog, k2, yo, k1, yo, k1, yo, k2, k2tog*; rep * to * around.
Rnd 6: K3, *ssk, ssk, k7*; rep * to * around, ending with ssk, ssk, k4.
Rnd 7: *K2tog, (k1, yo) 4 times, k1, ssk*; rep * to * around.
Rnd 8: K2, *ssk, ssk, ssk, k5*; rep * to * around, ending with ssk, ssk, ssk, k3.
Rnd 9: *K2tog, (yo, k1) 4 times, yo, ssk*; rep * to * around.
Rnd 10: K1, *ssk, ssk, ssk, ssk, k3*; rep * to * around, ending with ssk, ssk, ssk, ssk, k2.
There are now 56 sts around.
Rnd 11: Knit, increasing around as evenly spaced as possible to 95 sts.
Rnd 12: Purl.
Rnd 13: *K2tog, yo*; rep * to * around
Rnd 14: Knit.
Rnd 15: Purl.
Rnd 16: Knit.
Continue to leg.

Without Lace Edging

With Natural White, CO 96 sts. Divide sts evenly onto 4 dpn. Join, being careful not to twist cast-on row. Pm for beginning of rnd and work around in k2, p2 ribbing for 1½ in / 4 cm. Decrease 1 st at center back.

LEG, BOTH SIZES

Work following the Leg Chart = 81 sts rem at completion of chart.

COMMON HEEL

After completing sock leg, place 43 sts on a holder (see chart) for instep. These sts will "rest" until the heel is finished.

Heel Flap

Divide the remaining 38 stitches onto two dpn (Ndls A and B) and work back and forth with Natural White. Begin with the RS facing you. **NOTE:** On the first row only, decrease 1 st at the center of each needle = 18 sts rem on each dpn.
Row 1 (RS): Sl 1 purlwise wyb, knit all sts on Ndls A and B.
Row 2: Sl 1 purlwise wyf, purl all sts on Ndls A and B.
Repeat these 2 rows until there are 13 chain sts at each side of the flap.

Shaping the Heel

Now you will shape the back by decreasing as follows:
Row 1: Sl 1, knit until 5 sts rem on Ndl A, k2tog, k3. On Ndl B, k3, ssk, knit to end of needle.
Row 2: Sl 1, purl to end of row.
Row 3: Sl 1, knit until 4 sts rem on Ndl A, k2tog, k2. On Ndl B, k2, ssk, knit to end of needle.
Row 4: Sl 1, purl to end of row.
Row 5: Sl 1, knit until 3 sts rem on Ndl A, k2tog, k1. On Ndl B, k1, ssk, knit to end of needle.
Row 6: Sl 1, purl to end of row.
Row 7: Sl 1, knit until 2 sts rem on Ndl A, k2tog. On Ndl B, ssk, knit to end of needle.
Row 8: Sl 1, purl to end of Ndl B. Yarn is now at center of heel flap.
Hold the two dpn with RS facing in (so WS faces out on each side). Join the sets of sts with 3-needle BO: K2tog with 1 st from each needle, *k2tog with next st from each needle, pass first st over the second*. Repeat from * to * until 1 st loop rem.

Divide the instep sts onto 2 dpn. With RS facing, Natural White (carrying Blue), and Ndl 1, beginning at the center of the sole, pick up and knit 1 st in each chain st on the side of the flap. You can pick up the chain sts through back loops or knit them tbl on the next rnd. Work the instep sts on Ndls 2-3, in pattern following the chart. With Ndl 4, pick up and knit sts on opposite side of heel flap = 78 sts total.

FOOT

Work foot following the foot chart to desired length before toe.

STAR TOE

Begin at the center of the sole.
Rnd 1: (K5, k2tog) around. The 1 st rem on Ndl 4 will be decreased in subsequent rnds.
Rnds 2-6: Knit.
Rnd 7: (K4, k2tog) around.
Rnds 8-11: Knit.
Rnd 12: (K3, k2tog) around.
Rnds 13-15: Knit
Rnd 16: (K2, k2tog) around.
Rnds 17-18: Knit.
Rnd 19: (K1, k2tog) around.
Rnd 20: Knit.
Rnd 21: (K2tog) around.

FINISHING

Cut yarn and draw end through rem sts; tighten. Weave in all ends neatly on WS. Make the second sock the same way.

See page 22 for how to finish and block the lace edging so it looks good, if you chose to include it.

King of the Forest Mittens

Moose, deer, and reindeer on Norwegian knitted garments are practically national symbols. For example, Annichen Sibbern Bøhn has a large stag with impressive antlers in her book *Norwegian Knitting Patterns*, which came out in 1928. I let myself be inspired by many of the enjoyable animal motifs, but have chosen to use a tighter and more stylized form for my moose.

INSTRUCTIONS
Sizes: Women's (Men's)

MATERIALS
Yarn:
CYCA #1 (fingering) 2-ply Gammelserie from Rauma (100% wool, 175 yd/160 m / 50 g), Gray 405: 50 (100) g
CYCA #1 (light fingering) Lamullgarn from Rauma (100% wool (273 yd/250 m / 50 g), White L11: 50 (100) g
Needles: U.S. size 1.5 (2.5) / 2.5 (3) mm, set of 5 dpn
Gauge: 32 (29) sts = 4 in / 10 cm.
Adjust needle size to obtain correct gauge if necessary.

RIGHT MITTEN
With White, CO 60 sts and divide sts evenly over 4 dpn. Join to work in the round. Work around in k1, p1 ribbing for 3¼ in / 8.5 cm). After ribbing is complete, change to St st, increase 1 st to 61 sts, and continue in St st following charted pattern. Increase as shown for the thumb gusset. At dark line, set aside 16 sts for the thumb (see page 15 for details). Continue, shaping top of mitten as shown on chart (see page 13 for details). Cut yarn and draw end through rem sts; tighten.

THUMB
Pick up and knit 18 + 18 sts around thumbhole = 36 sts total (see page 15). Divide sts onto 4 dpn and work as shown on thumb chart. Cut yarn and draw end through rem sts; tighten.

LEFT MITTEN
Work mirror-image from chart.

FINISHING
Weave in all ends neatly on WS.
Gently steam press under a damp pressing cloth to block.

Thumb:

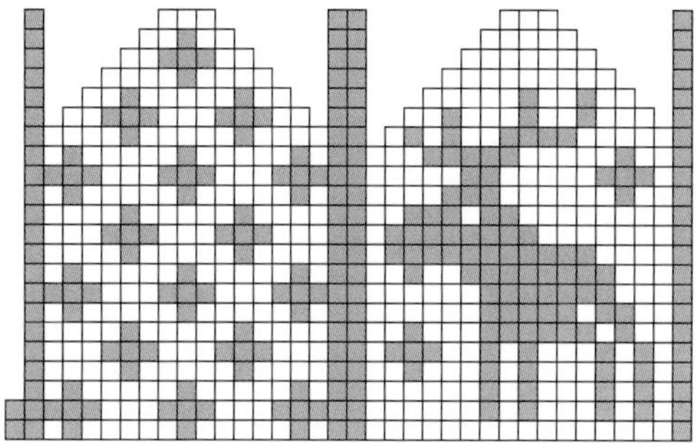

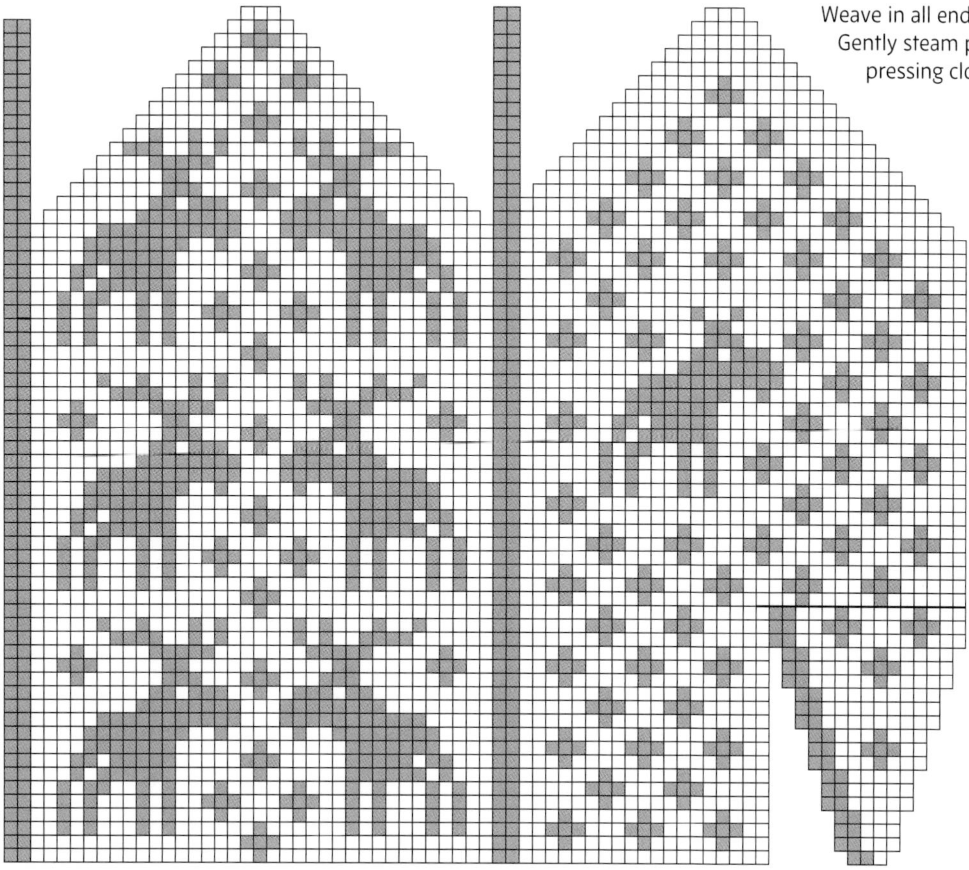

Set aside 16 sts for thumb.

☐ White—knit
■ Gray—knit

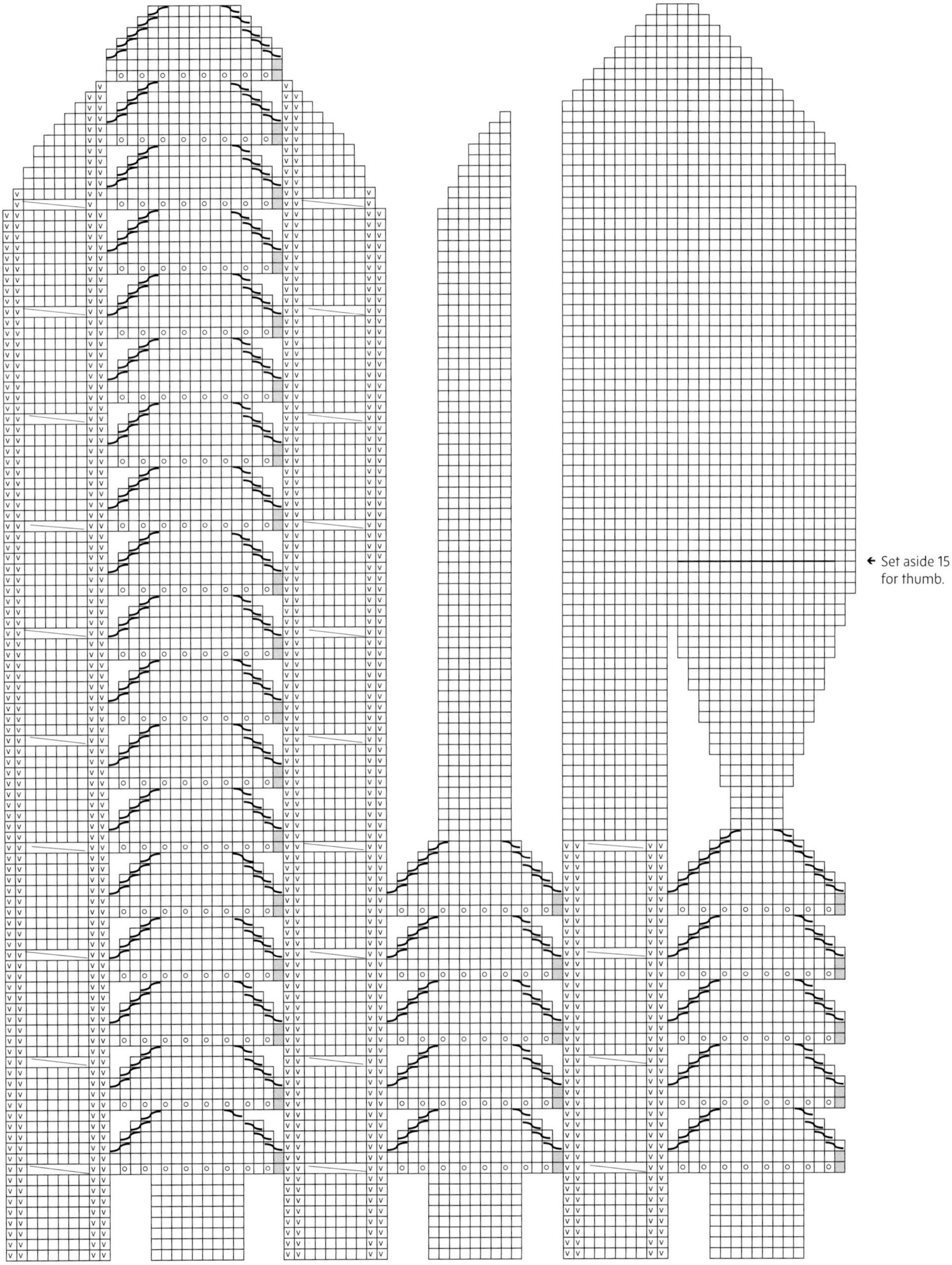
Set aside 15 sts for thumb.

Caroline Halvorsen's Mittens

Caroline Halvorsen's *Knitting Book for Schools and Home* came out in 1901; it was the first instructional knitting book in Norway, and was the basis for all knitting instruction in Norwegian schools until the 1950s and '60s. Mittens embellished with cables and fans were usually called "bride's mittens" or "church mittens," and, eventually, "Sunday mittens." Caroline Halvorsen didn't write complete instructions for the mittens, but described how to make the cables and fans. This is my variation on this type of mitten.

INSTRUCTIONS
Sizes: Women's

MATERIALS
Yarn:
CYCA #2 (sport) Ask (Hifa 2) from Hillesvåg Ullvarefabrikk (100% wool, 345 yd/315 m / 100 g), Golden Yellow 6094: 100 g
Needles: U.S. size 1.5 / 2.5 mm, set of 5 dpn
Gauge: 26 sts = 4 in / 10 cm.
Adjust needle size to obtain correct gauge if necessary.

RIGHT MITTEN
CO 57 sts and divide sts over dpn. Join to work in the round. Knit around in stockinette for ¾ in / 2 cm. Make an eyelet rnd: (k2tog, yo) around. Now work following the chart, increasing as shown. At dark line on chart, set aside 15 sts for thumbhole (see page 15 for details). Above the thumbhole, work the palm in St st and the back of the hand in lace and cable pattern as on the chart. Shape the top as indicated on the chart (see page 13 for details). Cut yarn and draw end through rem sts; tighten.

THUMB:

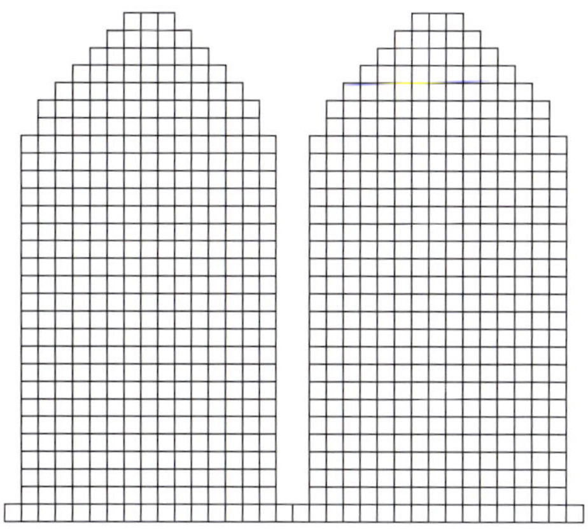

THUMB
Pick up and knit 17 + 17 sts around thumbhole = 34 sts total (see page 15). Divide sts onto 4 dpn and work as shown on thumb chart. Cut yarn and draw end through rem sts; tighten.

LEFT MITTEN
Work mirror-image from chart.

FINISHING
Weave in all ends neatly on WS. Gently steam press under a damp pressing cloth to block.

- knit
- purl
- twisted knit (= k1tbl)
- yo
- k2tog tbl or ssk
- k2tog
- sl 3 sts to a cable needle and hold in front of work, k3, k3 from cable needle

□ Light Turquoise—knit
■ Blue—knit
▣ Blue—purl
⊡ CO 1 st with Light Turquoise
▪ CO 1 st with Blue

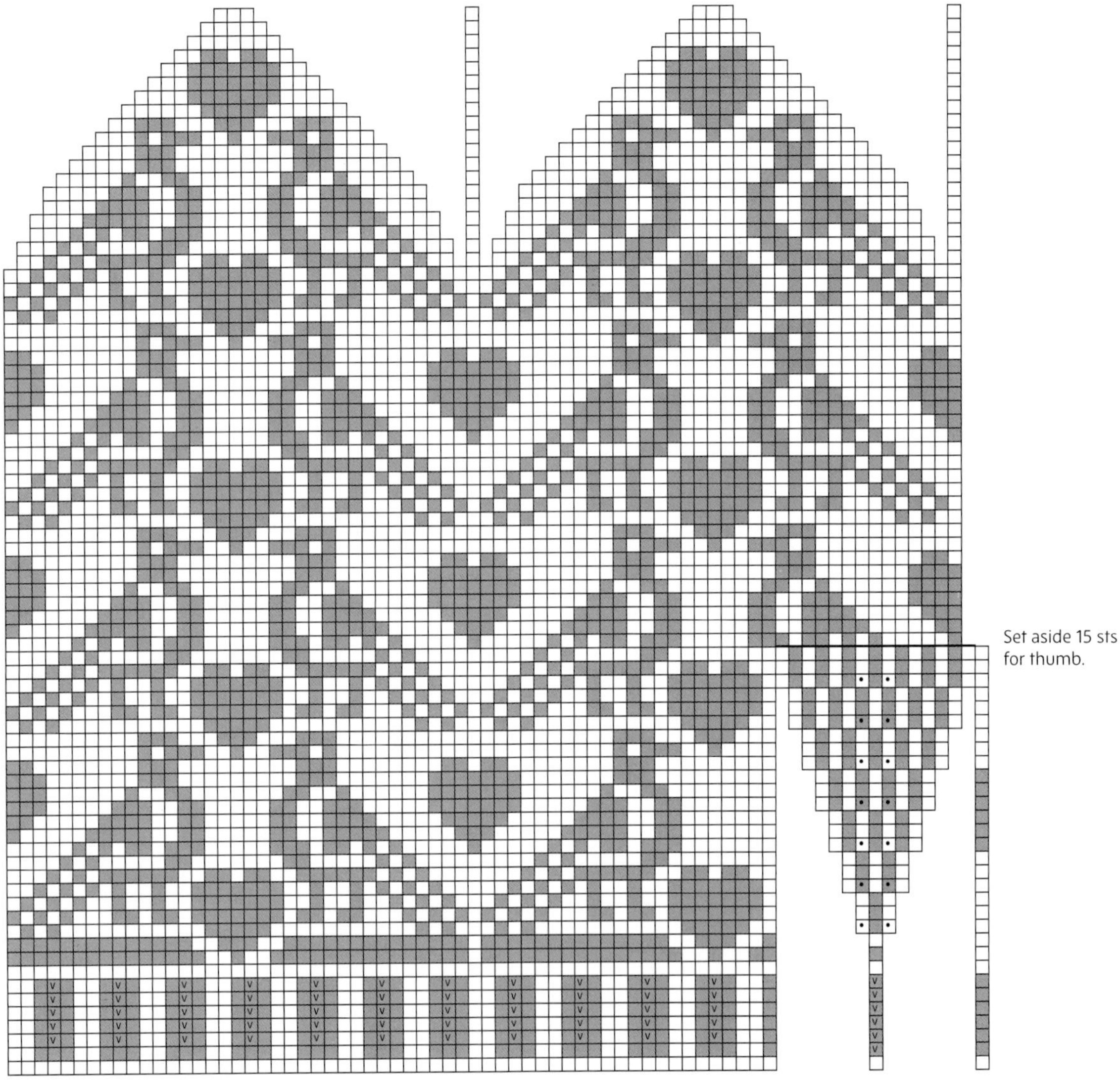

Thumb:

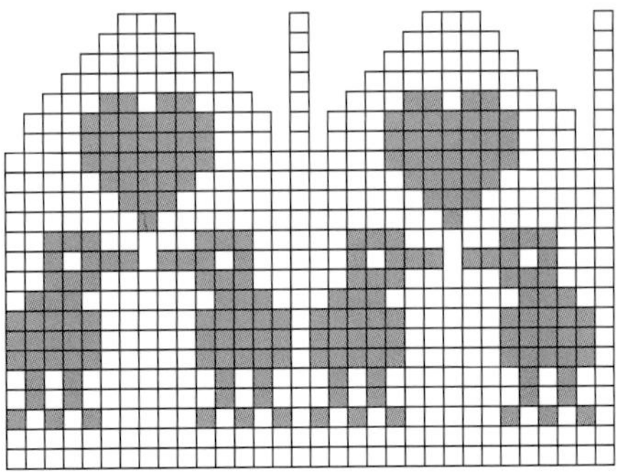

Love Mittens

A heart and two birds with beaks facing each other are both ancient symbols of love. These mittens are knitted in a lovely soft yarn that almost caresses the hands, and they're among my top favorites.

INSTRUCTIONS
Sizes: Women's (Men's)

MATERIALS
Yarn:
CYCA #1 (light fingering) Mari from Telespinn (80% mohair, 20% Merino wool, 190 yd/174 m / 50 g): Light Turquoise M322: 50 (100) g
CYCA #2 (sport) Arroyo from Malabrigo Yarn (100% Merino wool, 334 yd/305 m / 100 g): Azules 856 (blue heather): 50 (100) g
For the blue Malabrigo, you can substitute CYCA #1 (fingering) Dale Baby Ull (100% Merino wool, 180 yd/165 m / 50 g): Blue 5545
Needles: U. S. size 1.5 (2.5) / 2.5 (3) mm: set of 5 dpn
Gauge: 30 (28) sts in pattern = 4 in / 10 cm. Adjust needle size to obtain correct gauge if necessary.

RIGHT MITTEN
With Turquoise, CO 60 sts. Divide sts evenly onto 4 dpn and join. Knit 1 rnd. Change to Blue.
Rnd 1: *K2tog, k2, yo, k1, yo, k2, k2tog tbl, k1*; rep * to * around.
Rnd 2: Knit around.
Rep Rnds 1-2 a total of 8 times.

Now work following chart, increasing as shown. At dark line, place 15 sts on a holder for thumb. CO 13 new sts over gap.

Continue following chart, decreasing as shown for top.
When decreasing on right side of mitten, sl 1, k1, psso.
When decreasing on left side of mitten, k2tog.

THUMB
Pick up 16 + 16 sts = 32 sts total.
Work thumb following chart, shaping top as shown. Cut yarn, draw end through rem sts, and tighten.

LEFT MITTEN
Work mirror-image from chart.

FINISHING
Weave in all ends neatly on WS. Gently steam press under a damp pressing cloth to block.

Stockings from Valdres

A collection from the parish of Bagn includes a pair of bride's stockings worn by Sigrid Hansdatter Islandsmoen from Søndre Aurdal. They were knitted with white cotton yarn and feature a wide panel of pink-red patterning on the legs. Here is the same pattern on a pair of socks.

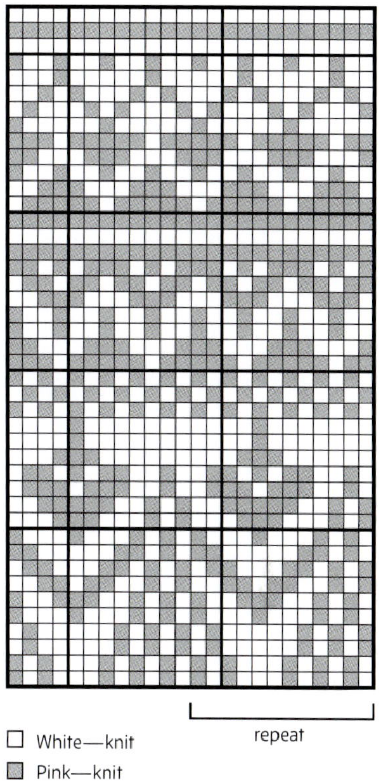

INSTRUCTIONS
Sizes: Women's (Men's)

MATERIALS
Yarn:
CYCA #1 (fingering) Sisu from Sandnes Garn (80% wool, 20% nylon), 191 yd/175 m / 50 g)
Yarn Colors and Amounts:
White 1012: 100 (100) g
Pink 4627: 50 (50) g
Needles: U. S. size 1.5 (2.5) / 2.5 (3) mm: set of 5 dpn
Gauge: 32 (30) sts in pattern = 4 in / 10 cm.
Adjust needle size to obtain correct gauge if necessary.

LEG
With White, CO 76 sts. Divide sts evenly onto 4 dpn. Join, being careful not to twist cast-on row; pm for beginning of rnd. Work around in k2, p1 ribbing for 2 in / 5 cm. Change to stockinette, and, on the first rnd, decrease 2 sts at the center back. Work in stockinette for ¾ in / 2 cm. Decrease another 2 sts at center back and knit another ⅜ in / 1 cm = 72 sts rem. Work remainder of leg in charted pattern.

BAND HEEL
After completing leg, place 36 sts on a holder for the instep (to "rest" while you work the heel flap).

Heel Flap
Place rem 36 sts on one dpn and, with White, work heel flap back and forth.

Begin with WS facing you.
Row 1 (WS): Sl 1 purlwise wyf, purl to end of row.
Row 2: Sl 1 purlwise wyb, knit to end of row.
Rep these 2 rows until there are 18 chain sts at each side of flap.

Now decrease to shape the band:
Row 1: Sl 1, purl until 12 sts rem, p2tog; turn.
Row 2: Sl 1, knit until 12 sts rem, ssk; turn.
Row 3: Sl 1, purl until 1 st before gap, p2tog; turn.
Row 4: Sl 1, knit until 1 st before gap, ssk; turn.
Rep Rows 3-4 until all the side sts have been eliminated.

FOOT
Divide the instep sts onto 2 dpn and divide the rem heel sts onto 2 dpn so you have half of each section on a needle. Work in the round with RS facing you. Begin rnd at center of sole. Pick up and knit 1 st in each chain st along side of heel flap. You can pick up the sts tbl or knit them tbl on next rnd. Knit across instep. Pick up and knit 1 st in each chain st of opposite side of flap and knit to end of rnd.

Gusset
Knit until 2 sts rem on Ndl 1, k2tog. Knit across instep (Ndls 2-3). Ndl 4: Ssk, knit to end of rnd. Knit the next rnd without decreasing. Rep these 2 rnds until 72 sts rem. Work rest of foot in stockinette without shaping until 7½ in / 19 cm or desired length before toe.

STAR TOE
Begin at the center of the sole and work only with Natural White.
Rnd 1: (K5, k2tog) around. The 2 sts rem on Ndl 4 will be decreased in subsequent rnds.
Rnds 2-6: Knit.
Rnd 7: (K4, k2tog) around.
Rnds 8-11: Knit.
Rnd 12: (K3, k2tog) around.
Rnds 13-15: Knit
Rnd 16: (K2, k2tog) around.
Rnds 17-18: Knit.
Rnd 19: (K1, k2tog) around.
Rnd 20: Knit.
Rnd 21: (K2tog) around.

FINISHING
Cut yarn and draw end through rem sts; tighten. Weave in all ends neatly on WS. Make the second sock the same way.

- ☐ White—knit
- ■ Red—knit
- ☑ White—purl
- ▣ Red—purl

Thumb:

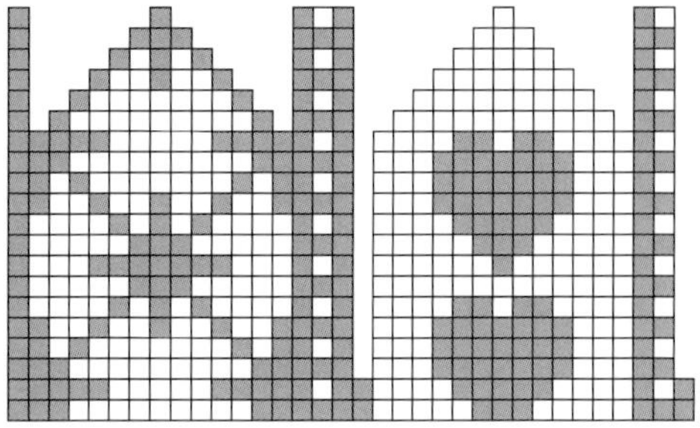

Heart Brooch Mittens

The pattern for these mittens was inspired by an elegant heart brooch. Heart brooches have been used to decorate folk costumes all around Norway, although the shape varies quite a bit from province to province. Brooches were often decorated with a crown at the top. It's also common to find a crown over a heart on old samplers—where it was a symbol of devotion.

INSTRUCTIONS
Sizes: Women's (Men's)

MATERIALS
Yarn:
CYCA #1 (fingering) Dale Baby Ull (100% Merino wool, 180 yd/165 m / 50 g)
Yarn Amounts:
Red 4018: 50 (100) g
White 0010: 50 (100) g
Needles: U.S. size 0 (1.5) / 2 (2.5) mm, set of 5 dpn
Gauge: 35 (32) sts = 4 in / 10 cm. Adjust needle size to obtain correct gauge if necessary.

RIGHT MITTEN
With Red, CO 64 sts and divide sts evenly over 4 dpn. Join to work in the round. Work 2 rnds of staggered ribbing as shown on the chart. Change to White and continue staggered rib as charted. After completing ribbing, continue in St st and pattern following the chart.

Increase for the thumb gusset as shown and, at the dark line, place the 16 thumb sts on a holder. CO 15 sts over the gap on the next rnd.

Continue, shaping top of mitten as shown on chart (see page 13 for details). Cut yarn and draw end through rem sts; tighten.

THUMB
Pick up and knit 17 + 17 sts around thumbhole = 34 sts total. Divide sts onto 4 dpn and work as shown on thumb chart. Cut yarn and draw end through rem sts; tighten.

LEFT MITTEN
Work mirror-image from chart.

FINISHING
Weave in all ends neatly on WS. Gently steam press under a damp pressing cloth to block.

Thumb:

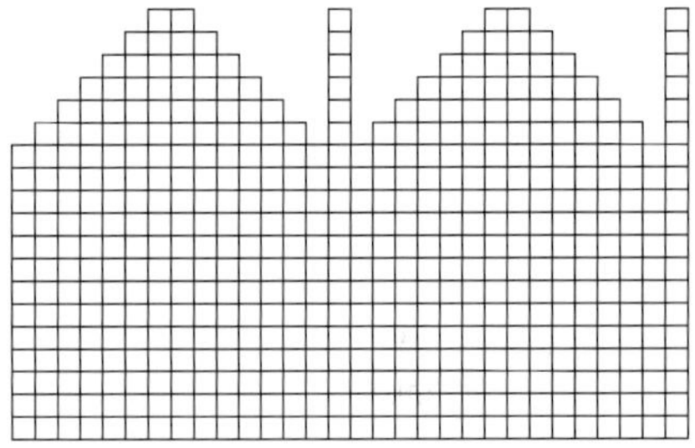

- □ White—knit
- ■ Blue—knit
- ☑ White—purl
- ▣ Blue—purl

← Set aside 13 sts for thumb.

Porcelain Flower Mittens

Historically, if you wanted to dye some wool blue, you had to use a plant called woad, or authentic indigo from *indigofera anil*, introduced from the tropics. Synthetic indigo came on the market in about 1900. The blue color used to decorate porcelain was derived from cobalt. The highest quality of this dye powder was sent from the Blue Dye Works in Modum in Buskerud to customers all over the world. These mittens were inspired by the blue flowers often seen on Danish, German, and Norwegian porcelain.

INSTRUCTIONS
Sizes: Women's (Men's)

MATERIALS
Yarn:
CYCA #2 (sport) PT5 from Rauma (80% wool, 20% polyamide, 140 yd/128 m / 50 g)
Yarn Amounts
Blue 567: 50 (100) g
White 502: 50 (100) g
Needles: U.S. size 2.5 (4) / 3 (3.5) mm, set of 5 dpn
Gauge: 27 (24) sts = 4 in / 10 cm. Adjust needle size to obtain correct gauge if necessary.

NOTE: This design has long yarn floats. For best results, you should twist the white and blue strands around each other on the wrong side on about every sixth stitch.
On the next round, stagger the twist to the left or to the right to avoid stacking the twists above each other. Stacked yarn twists will show through on the right side.

RIGHT MITTEN
With White, CO 60 sts. Divide sts over 4 dpn and join to work in the round. Knit 1 rnd and then purl 1 rnd. Continue with knit and purl sts as indicated on the chart.

Increase for the thumb gusset as indicated on chart. At the dark line, set aside 13 sts for the thumb (see page 15 for details).

Continue, shaping top of mitten as shown on chart (see page 13 for details). Cut yarn and draw end through rem sts; tighten.

THUMB
With White, pick up and knit 30 sts around thumbhole. Divide sts onto 4 dpn and work as shown on thumb chart. Cut yarn and draw end through rem sts; tighten.

LEFT MITTEN
Work mirror-image from chart.

FINISHING
Weave in all ends neatly on WS. Gently steam press under a damp pressing cloth to block.

Thumb:

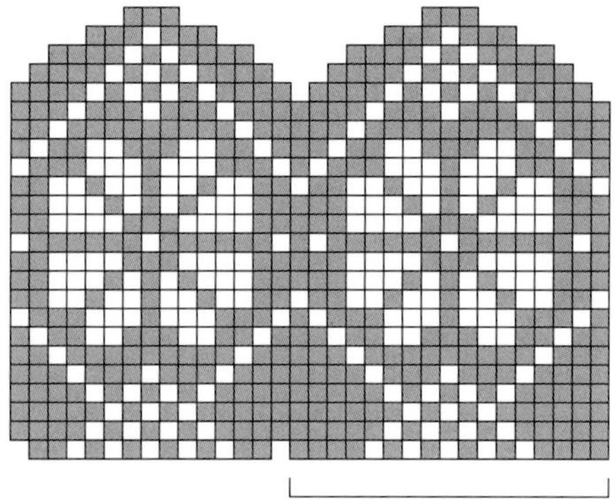

front of thumb.

Red—knit

White—knit

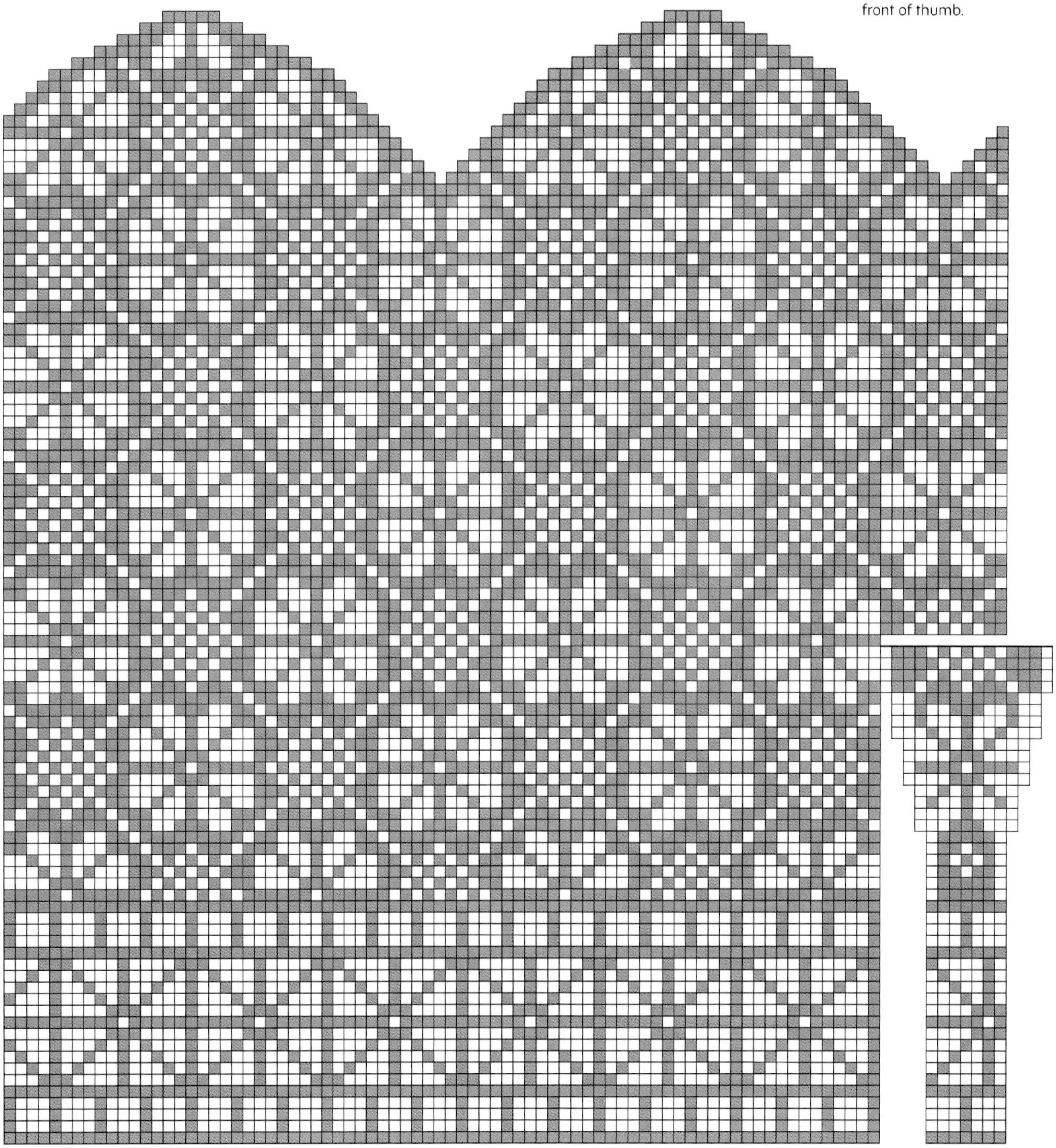

Set aside 15 sts for thumb.

Rose Mittens from Skjåk

Among the items registered in connection with the exhibition "Knitting Then and Now" in 1984 are a pair of men's mittens from Skjåk, which are locally called "rose mittens." They were knitted with black and white handspun yarn. This rose pattern was knitted by multiple women in Skjåk.

INSTRUCTIONS
Sizes: Women's (Men's)

MATERIALS
Yarn:
CYCA #1 (fingering) Dale Baby Ull (100% Merino wool, 180 yd/165 m / 50 g)
Yarn Amounts
Red 4018: 50 (100) g
White 0017: 50 (100) g
Needles: U.S. size 0 (1.5) / 2 (2.5) mm, set of 5 dpn
Gauge: 38 (34) sts = 4 in / 10 cm. Adjust needle size to obtain correct gauge if necessary.

RIGHT MITTEN
With Red over the thumb and White over index finger, use the long-tail method to CO 84 sts and divide sts evenly over 4 dpn. Join to work in the round. Work 1 rnd two-end purl braid (see page 14). Continue in St st following the chart.

Increase for the thumb gusset as shown and, at the dark line, place the 15 thumb sts on a holder. CO 11 sts over the gap on the next rnd.

Continue, shaping top of mitten as shown on chart (see page 13 for details). Cut yarn and draw end through rem sts; tighten.

THUMB
Pick up and knit 17 + 13 sts around thumbhole = 30 sts total. Divide sts onto 4 dpn and work in St st as shown on thumb chart. On the second rnd, inc 2 sts on the back of the thumb as indicated on chart. Cut yarn and draw end through rem sts; tighten.

LEFT MITTEN
Work mirror-image from chart.

FINISHING
Weave in all ends neatly on WS. Gently steam press under a damp pressing cloth to block.

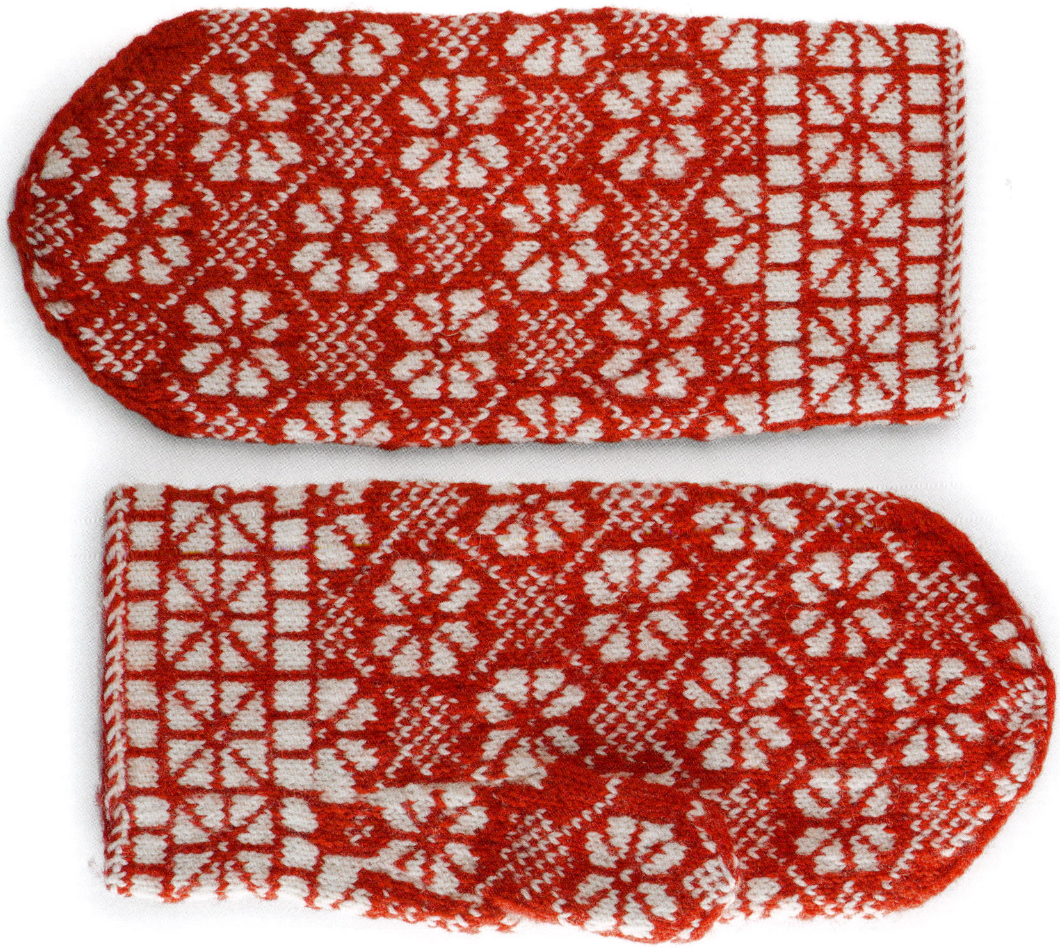

ÅSNES
ÅSNES

□ Blue—knit
□ Natural White—knit

Chart 4

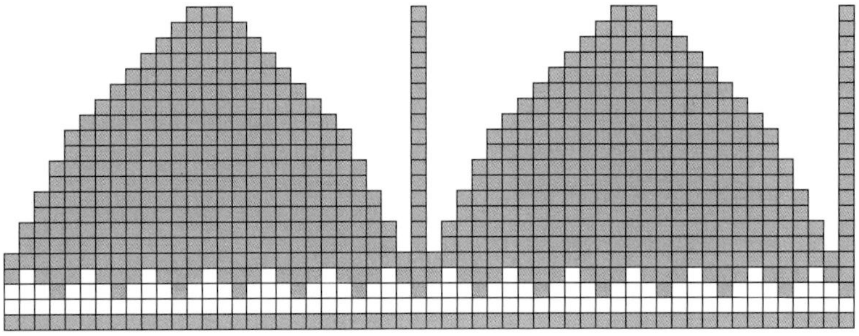

Chart 3

Set aside 11 sts for thumb.

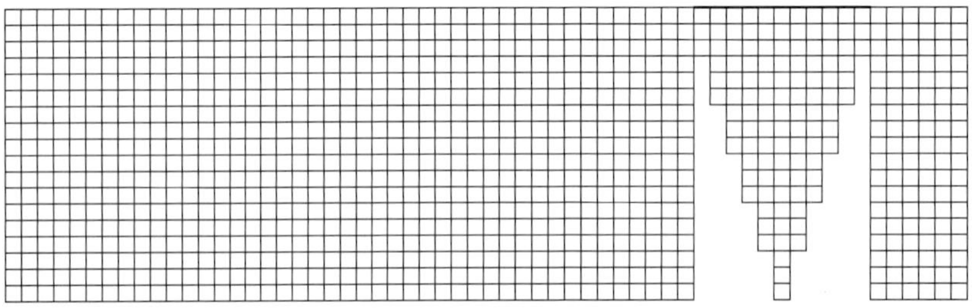

Chart 2

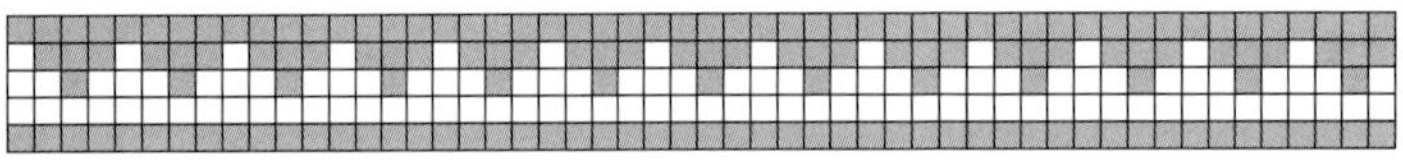

Chart 1

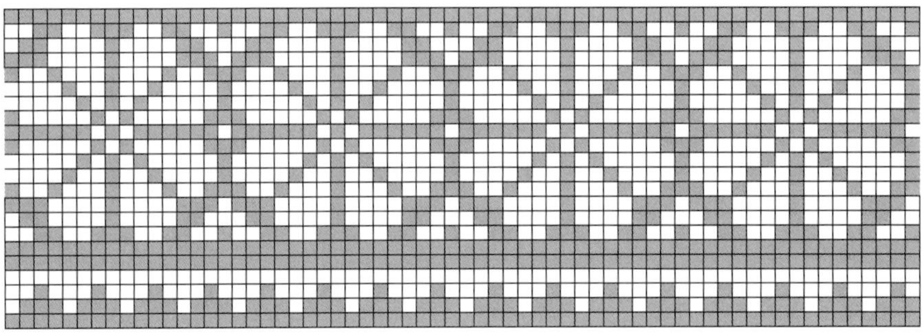

Thumb:

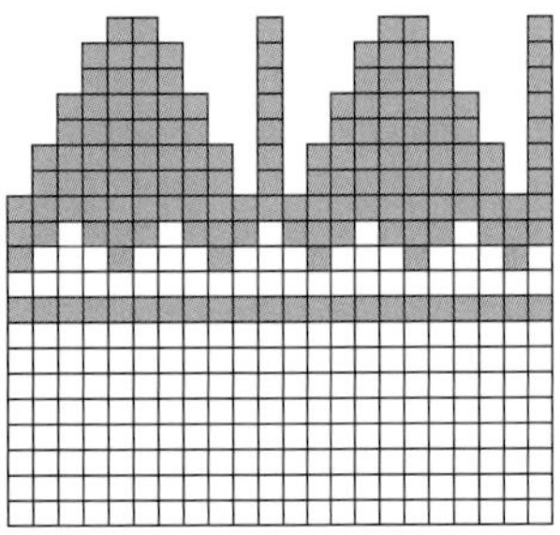

Blue Monday Mittens

These mittens have a little pattern on the cuffs, but it's easy to knit. So this is a good knitting project for early in the week—when you don't want to have to think too hard on a Monday.

INSTRUCTIONS
Sizes: Women's (Men's)

MATERIALS
Yarn: CYCA #3 (DK, light worsted) Sterk from Du Store Alpakka (40% alpaca, 40% Merino wool, 20% polyamide, 150 yd/137 m / 50 g)
Yarn Amounts
Natural 806: 50 (50) g
Blue 815: 50 (100) g
Needles: U.S. size 2.5 (4) / 3 (3.5) mm, set of 5 dpn
Gauge: 25 (23) sts = 4 in / 10 cm. Adjust needle size to obtain correct gauge if necessary.

RIGHT MITTEN
With Blue, CO 64 sts and divide sts evenly over 4 dpn. Join to work in the round. Knit 4 rnds. Purl 1 rnd and then continue in stockinette following Chart 1. Knit 1 rnd, decreasing to 52 sts evenly spaced around. Work following Chart 2, and on the last rnd, decrease another 2 sts = 50 sts rem.

Continue in stockinette with Natural, at the same time increasing for thumb gusset as shown on Chart 3. It will look nicest if you align the thumb so it's centered on a flower. Make sure it aligns with regard to the shaping. Increase as shown to a total of 60 sts, and then knit 2 more rnds.

Place 11 sts on a holder. CO 7 new sts over the gap = a total of 56 sts. Divide sts over 4 dpn = 14 sts per needle.

Continue in stockinette with Natural until mitten reaches nail of little finger. Change to Blue and work in pattern following Chart 4, shaping top as shown. Decrease on left side of mitten with k2tog. Decrease on right side with sl 1, k1 psso. When 8 sts rem, cut yarn and draw end through rem sts; tighten.

THUMB
Pick up and knit 13 sts on front + 9 sts on back = 22 sts total. Divide sts over 4 dpn = 5 + 6 + 5 + 6 sts. Work in St st as shown on thumb chart. Shape top as for mitten top. When 6 sts rem, cut yarn and draw end through rem sts; tighten.

LEFT MITTEN
Work mirror-image from chart.

FINISHING
Weave in all ends neatly on WS. Gently steam press under a damp pressing cloth to block.

Thumb:

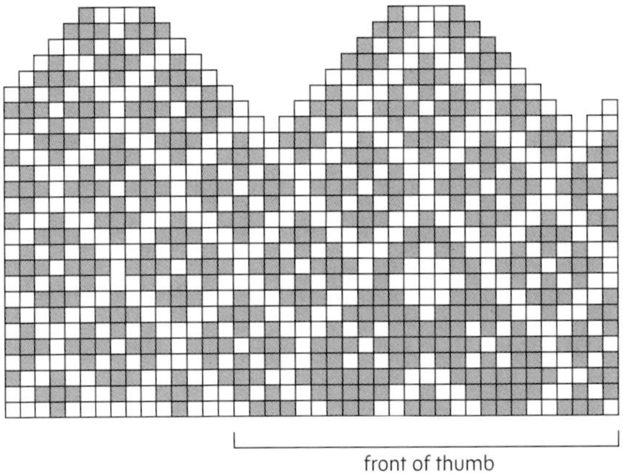

☐ White—knit
▩ Gray—knit

Mittens from Hallingdal

Hallingdal Museum has a pair of mittens from Knut Knutson Heje of Flå. The mittens were knitted with a strong 3-ply handspun wool yarn in natural black and white, and embellished with a fringe around the wrist. On the outer side of the cuffs, the initials KKSH are knitted in. I chose to make mittens following the same pattern, but without the initials or the fringe.

INSTRUCTIONS
Sizes: Women's (Men's)

MATERIALS
Yarn:
CYCA #1 (fingering) two-ply Spelsau from Hoelfeldt-Lund (100% wool, 244 yd/223 m / 50 g) OR Norsk Pelsull from Hillesvåg (CYCA #3 [DK/light worsted], 100% wool, 284 yd/260 m / 100 g)
Yarn Amounts
Dark Gray (natural color): 100 (100) g
Light Gray (natural color): 100 (100) g
Needles: U.S. size 0 (1.5) / 2 (2.5) mm, set of 5 dpn
Gauge: 34 (31) sts = 4 in / 10 cm. Adjust needle size to obtain correct gauge if necessary.

RIGHT MITTEN
With Dark Gray over the thumb and Light Gray over the index finger, use the long-tail cast-on method to CO 72 sts. Divide sts over 4 dpn and join to work in the round. Work 1 rnd two-end purl braid (see page 14). Continue in St st following the chart.

Increase for the thumb gusset as indicated on chart. At the dark line, place the 25 thumb sts on a holder. CO 10 sts over the gap on the next rnd.

Continue, shaping top of mitten as shown on chart (see page 13 for details). Cut yarn and draw end through rem sts; tighten.

THUMB
Pick up and knit 27 + 13 sts around thumbhole = 40 sts total. Make sure that the pattern is correctly aligned over the sts held for the thumb. Divide sts onto 4 dpn and work as shown on thumb chart. Cut yarn and draw end through rem sts; tighten.

LEFT MITTEN
Work mirror-image from chart.

FINISHING
Weave in all ends neatly on WS. Gently steam press under a damp pressing cloth to block.

Halling Socks

The pattern sequence on these socks is based on a pair of long stockings from Flå in Hallingdal. There, such stockings are called *hosurpar* or *hosu i tviband* ("two-end" *hosu*). In both Telemark and Buskerud, "two-end knitting" refers to ordinary pattern knitting with two strands (colorwork knitting), but in other parts of the country, it refers to the two-end knitting technique in which both strands are held on the right side to form patterns (also called "twined knitting" in English).

INSTRUCTIONS
Sizes: Women's (Men's)

MATERIALS
Yarn: CYCA #1 (fingering) Mini Sterk from Du Store Alpakka (40% alpaca, 40% Merino wool, 20% polyamide, 182 yd/166 m / 50 g)
Yarn Colors and Amounts:
Light Pink 850: 100 (100) g
Black 809: 50 (50) g
Needles: U. S. size 1.5 (2.5) / 2.5 (3) mm: set of 5 dpn
Gauge: 34 (32) sts in pattern = 4 in / 10 cm.
Adjust needle size to obtain correct gauge if necessary.

LEG
With Pink, CO 76 sts. Divide sts evenly onto 4 dpn. Join, being careful not to twist cast-on row; pm for beginning of rnd. Work in k2, p2 ribbing for 1½ in / 4 cm. On the last rnd, increase 1 st at center back. Now work in pattern following Chart 1. Work the repeat 4 times in length.

BAND HEEL
After completing leg, place 40 sts on a holder for the instep (to "rest" while you work the heel flap). Make sure the pattern is centered.

Heel Flap
Place rem 37 sts on one dpn and, with Pink, work heel flap back and forth. Begin with WS facing you.
Row 1 (WS): Sl 1 purlwise wyf, purl to last st.
Row 2: Sl 1 purlwise wyb, (k1, sl 1) to last st and end with k1.
Rep these 2 rows until there are 18 chain sts at each side of flap.

Now decrease to shape the band:
Row 1: Sl 1, purl until 12 sts rem, p2tog; turn.
Row 2: Sl 1, knit until 12 sts rem, ssk; turn.
Row 3: Sl 1, purl until 1 st before gap, p2tog; turn.
Row 4: Sl 1, knit until 1 st before gap, ssk; turn.
Rep Rows 3-4 until all the side sts have been eliminated.

FOOT
Divide the instep sts onto 2 dpn and divide the rem heel sts onto 2 dpn so you have half of each section on a needle. Work in the round with RS facing you.

Begin rnd at center of sole. Alternating Black and Pink, knit to heel flap. Pick up and knit 1 st in each chain st along side of heel flap. You can pick up the sts tbl or knit them tbl on next rnd. The last st should be Pink so that you have 2 Pink sts next to each other. Knit across instep in pattern as est. Beginning with Pink and alternating Black and Pink, pick up and knit 1 st in each chain st of opposite side of flap and then knit to end of rnd.

Gusset
Work sole with Pink over Black and Black over Pink as shown on Chart 2. Ndl 1 always ends with Pink and Ndl 4 always begins with Pink. Continue pattern on instep as est.

Knit until 2 sts rem on Ndl 1, k2tog. Work across instep (Ndls 2-3) in pattern. Ndl 4: Ssk, knit to end of rnd. Knit the next rnd without decreasing. Rep these 2 rnds until 77 sts rem. Work rest of foot in stockinette without shaping until 8 (9½) in / 20 (24) cm or desired length before toe.

STAR TOE
Begin at the center of the sole and work only with Pink.
Rnd 1: (K5, k2tog) around.
Rnds 2-6: Knit.
Rnd 7: (K4, k2tog) around.
Rnds 8-11: Knit.
Rnd 12: (K3, k2tog) around.
Rnds 13-15: Knit
Rnd 16: (K2, k2tog) around.
Rnds 17-18: Knit.
Rnd 19: (K1, k2tog) around.
Rnd 20: Knit.
Rnd 21: (K2tog) around.

FINISHING
Cut yarn and draw end through rem sts; tighten. Weave in all ends neatly on WS. Make the second sock the same way.

CHART 1

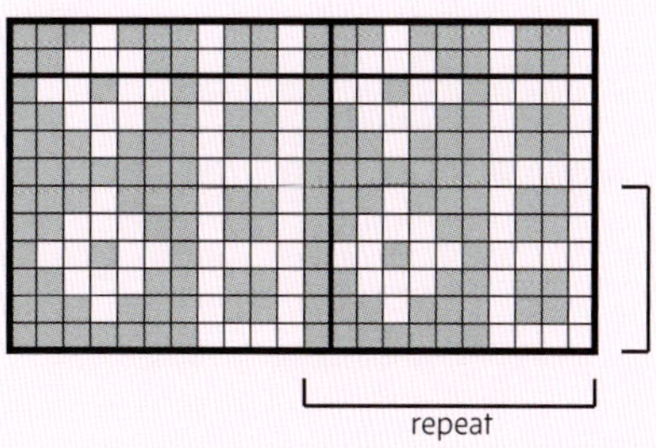

CHART 2

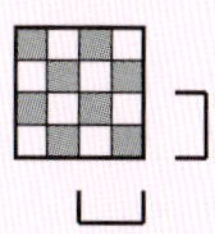

■ Black—knit
□ Pink—knit

Larvik Socks

Larvik Museum has a pair of children's stockings knitted with gray and white wool yarn, in stripes. The striping is worked by first knitting a certain number of rounds in stockinette with one color, and then knitting one round with a contrast color. The next round is purled with the contrast color. The technique is easy and a good choice for beginner knitters. I decided to use a hand-dyed flame yarn for the stripes, but another option would be to use a variety of leftover yarns.

INSTRUCTIONS
Sizes: Women's (Men's)

MATERIALS
Yarn:
CYCA #1 (fingering) Mini Sterk from Du Store Alpakka (40% alpaca, 40% Merino wool, 20% polyamide, 182 yd/166 m / 50 g), Gray 822 (MC): 100 (100) g
CYCA #1 (fingering) Superfine Merino/nylon Sock from The Happy Little Dye Pot (75% wool, 25% nylon, 437 yd / 400 m / 100 g), Hand-dyed (CC): 50 (50) g
Needles: U. S. 0 (1.5) / 2 (2.5) mm: set of 5 dpn
Gauge: 26 (28) sts in pattern = 4 in / 10 cm.
Adjust needle size to obtain correct gauge if necessary.

LEG
With Gray, CO 72 sts. Divide sts evenly onto 4 dpn. Join, being careful not to twist cast-on row; pm for beginning of rnd. Work in k2, p2 ribbing for 8 rnds.
Now work in pattern as follows:
*With Gray, knit 5 rnds in stockinette and then work pattern stripe.
With CC, knit 1 rnd.
With CC, purl 1 rnd.*
Rep * to * a total of 5 times.
Knit 1 rnd with Gray.
On the next rnd, decrease at center back: K2tog, knit until 2 sts rem, ssk.
Knit 3 more rnds with Gray and then work the 2-round pattern stripe.
Work this sequence with decreases a total of 3 times = 66 sts rem. Work 1 more pattern rep without decreasing and end with 5 rnds Gray.

BAND HEEL WITH SHORT HEEL FLAP
After completing leg, place 34 sts on a holder for the instep (to "rest" while you work the heel flap).

Heel Flap
Place rem 32 sts on one dpn and, with Gray, work reinforced heel flap back and forth.
Begin with WS facing you.
Row 1 (WS): Sl 1 purlwise wyf, purl to end of row.
Row 2: Sl 1 purlwise wyb, k1, sl 1 to last st and end with k1.
Rep these 2 rows until there are 11 chain sts at each side of flap.

Heel Gusset:
Row 1: Sl 1, purl until 12 sts rem, p2tog; turn.
Row 2: Sl 1, knit until 12 sts rem, ssk; turn.
Row 3: Sl 1, purl until 1 st before gap, p2tog; turn.
Row 4: Sl 1, knit until 1 st before gap, ssk; turn.
Rep Rows 3-4 until all the side sts have been eliminated = 10 sts rem.

FOOT
Divide the instep sts onto 2 dpn and divide the rem heel sts onto 2 dpn so you have half of each section on a needle. Work in the round with RS facing you.
Begin rnd at center of sole. With CC, k5. Pick up and knit 11 sts in chain sts along left side of heel flap. You can pick up the sts tbl or knit them tbl on next rnd. Knit across instep. Pick up and knit 11 sts in chain sts of opposite side of flap and then knit to end of rnd = 66 sts total. Purl the next rnd.

Work 7 (8) rep with Gray and dyed yarn pattern as est or to desired length before toe. Continue the pattern sequence while shaping the toe.

STAR TOE
Begin at the center of the sole.
Rnd 1: (K5, k2tog) around. The 3 sts rem at end of Ndl 4 will be decreased on the last 2 rounds.
Rnds 2-6: Knit.
Rnd 7: (K4, k2tog) around.
Rnds 8-11: Knit.
Rnd 12: (K3, k2tog) around.
Rnds 13-15: Knit
Rnd 16: (K2, k2tog) around.
Rnds 17-18: Knit.
Rnd 19: (K1, k2tog) around.
Rnd 20: Knit.
Rnd 21: (K2tog) around.

FINISHING
Cut yarn and draw end through rem sts; tighten. Weave in all ends neatly on WS. Make the second sock the same way.

FOOT

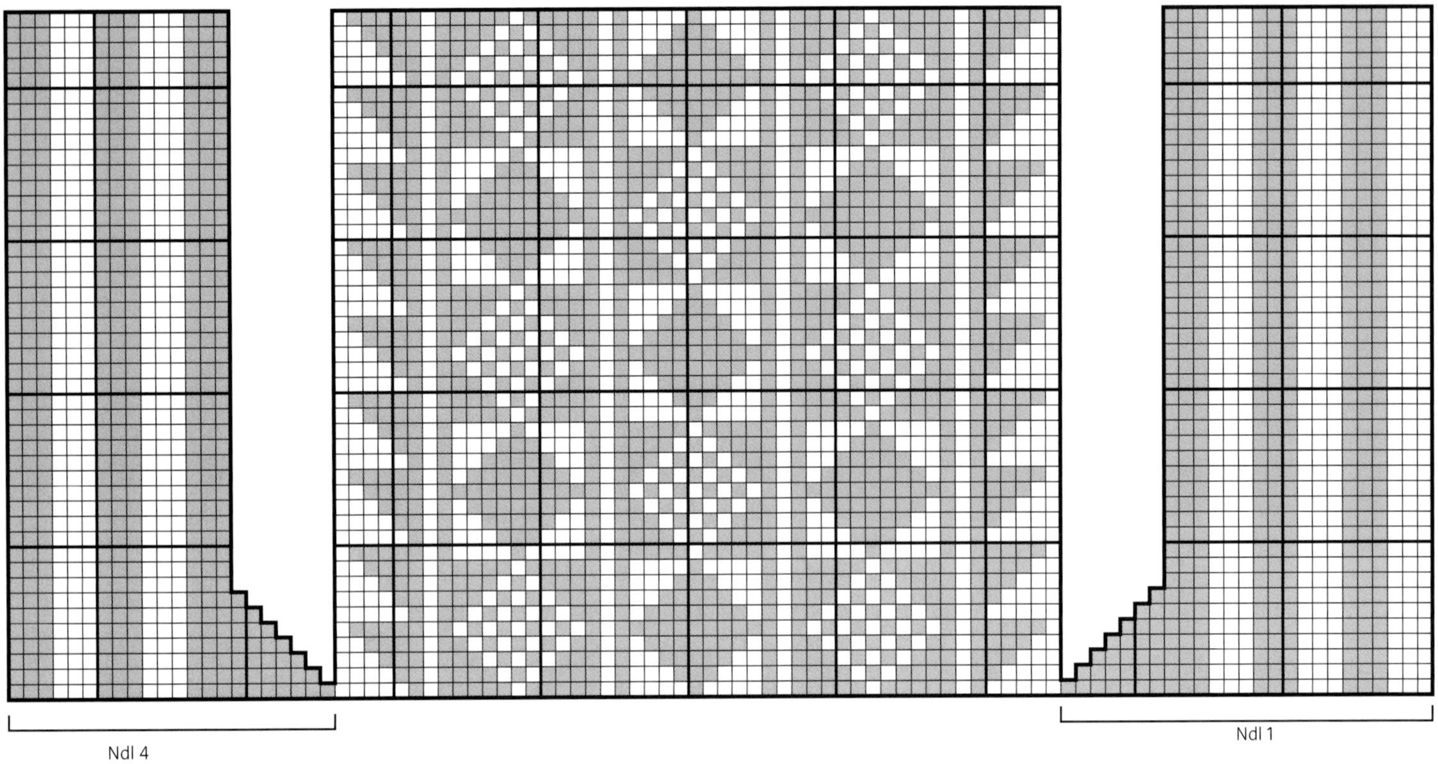

LEG

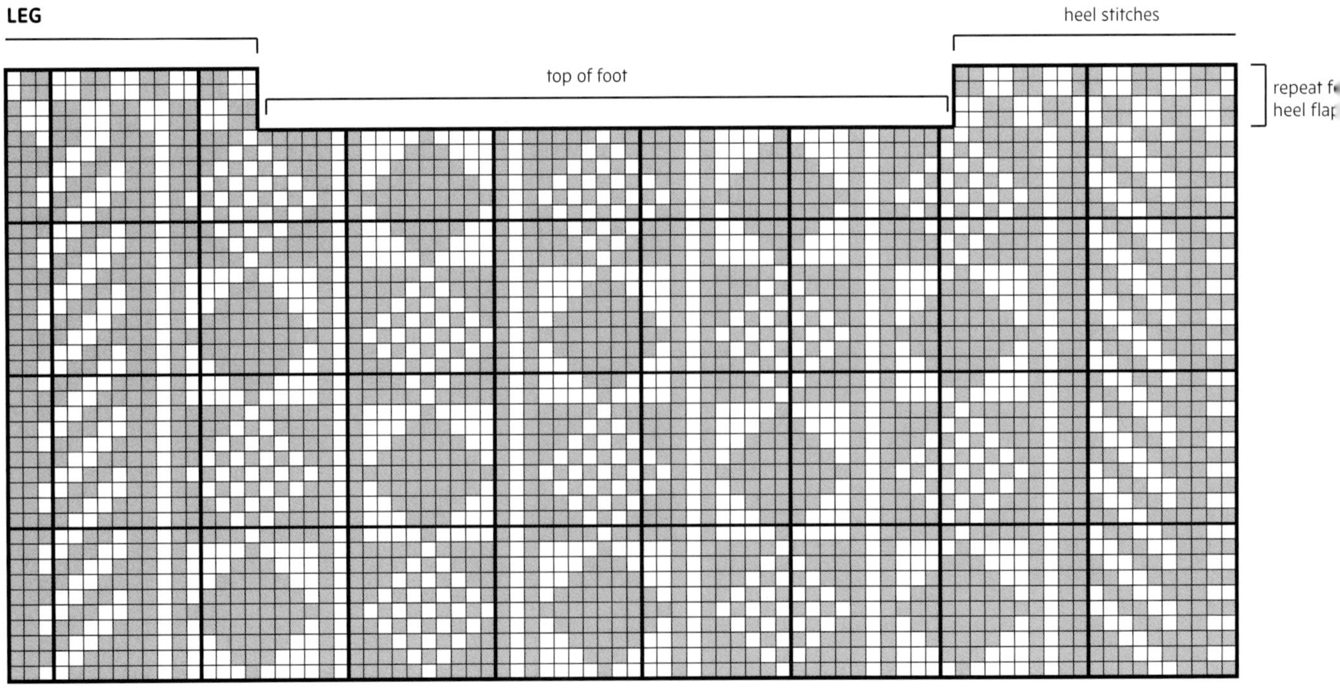

☐ Natural—knit
▩ Purple—knit

Telemark Socks

Norwegian museums have preserved several pairs of men's stockings from Telemark with characteristic block patterns in dark blue and sheep's natural white. The back of the calf features diagonally stylized stripes, while the ankles sport decorative eight-petal roses. Here is my short version of this style of stocking.

INSTRUCTIONS
Sizes: Women's (Men's)

MATERIALS
Yarn:
CYCA #1 (fingering) 2-ply Gammelserie from Rauma (100% wool, 175 yd/160 m / 50 g): Natural White 401, 100 (100) g
CYCA #0 (lace), Røros Embroidery yarn (Brodergarn) from Rauma Ullevarefabrikk (100% Spelsau wool): Purple 355, held double, 100 (100) g
Needles: U. S. size 0 (1.5) / 2 (2.5) mm: set of 5 dpn
Gauge: 34 (32) sts in pattern = 4 in / 10 cm.
Adjust needle size to obtain correct gauge if necessary.

LEG
With Natural White, CO 84 sts. Divide sts evenly onto 4 dpn. Join, being careful not to twist cast-on row; pm for beginning of rnd. Work in k3, p3 ribbing for 1¼ in / 3 cm. Next, knit 6 rnds in stockinette and, on the last rnd, decrease 1 st at center back—83 sts rem. Now work charted Leg pattern until you've completed 4 block tiers. Hold the Purple embroidery yarn double throughout.

GUSSET HEEL
After completing the leg, divide the stitches, placing the 47 instep sts onto scrap yarn. These instep stitches will "rest" until the heel is complete.

Heel Flap
Place the rem 36 sts onto one needle and work back and forth in checkerboard pattern as shown at top of Leg chart.
Begin with the WS facing you.
Row 1 (WS): Sl 1 purlwise wyf, purl to end of row.
Row 2: Sl 1 purlwise wyb, knit to end of row.
Work the first and last st of each row with both yarn colors together—White and Purple. Repeat these 2 rows until there are 12 chain sts at each side of the flap.

Shaping the Heel
With Natural White only:
Row 1: Sl 1, purl until 12 sts rem on the needle, p2tog, p1; turn.
Row 2: Sl 1, knit until 12 sts rem on needle, ssk, k1; turn.
Row 3: Sl 1, purl until 1 st before gap, p2tog, p1; turn.
Row 4: Sl 1, knit until 1 st rem before gap, ssk, k1; turn.
Repeat Rows 3–4 until all the side sts have been eliminated.

Gusset Shaping
Divide the instep sts from the holder onto 2 dpn; divide the sole sts onto 2 dpn with half of the sts on each. With RS facing, begin working in the round. Begin rnd at center of sole. With Ndl 1, k3 in Natural White as shown on chart. Continue with k3 Purple. When at side of heel flap, pick up and knit 1 st in each chain up side of flap. You can pick up the chain sts through back loops, or knit them through back loops on the next rnd.
NOTE: You need to carry both yarns here.
With Ndls 2-3, work across the instep in pattern as shown on chart. Next, with Ndl 4, pick up and knit sts in each chain st down opposite side of flap as for the first side. Knit to center of sole, increasing 1 st with M1 at end of rnd. Make sure the patterns match as you work around. You've now completed the first row of the foot chart and have 96 sts total.
On the next rnd, begin decreasing to shape gusset: Knit until 2 sts rem on Ndl 1, k2tog. Work across instep sts on Ndls 2–3 as shown on chart. On Ndl 4, ssk and then knit to end of rnd.
Work the next rnd without decreasing. Repeat these 2 rnds until 82 sts rem. Continue without further shaping, following charted pattern. Make sure the foot ends with a complete pattern repeat.

STAR TOE
Begin at the center of the sole with Natural White.
Rnd 1: (K5, k2tog) around. The 5 sts rem at end of Ndl 4 will be decreased on subsequent rnds.
Rnds 2–6: Knit.
Rnd 7: (K4, k2tog) around.
Rnds 8–11: Knit.
Rnd 12: (K3, k2tog) around.
Rnds 13-15: Knit
Rnd 16: (K2, k2tog) around.
Rnds 17–18: Knit.
Rnd 19: (K1, k2tog) around.
Rnd 20: Knit.
Rnd 21: (K2tog) around.

FINISHING
Cut yarn and draw end through rem sts; tighten. Weave in all ends neatly on WS. Make the second sock the same way.

Block Socks

You'll find block-patterned socks in several places in Norway. These socks were knitted in a simplified version with a decorative lace edging.

INSTRUCTIONS
Sizes: Women's S (Men's L)

MATERIALS
Yarn:
CYCA #0 (lace) Røros Embroidery yarn (Brodergarn) from Rauma Ullevare-fabrikk (100% Spelsau wool): Pink 346, held double, 50 (50) g
CYCA #1 (fingering) 2-ply Gammelserie from Rauma (100% wool, 175 yd/160 m / 50 g): Red 424: 50 (50) g
Natural White 401, 50 (50) g
Needles: U. S. size 1.5 (2.5) / 2.5 (3) mm: set of 5 dpn
Gauge: 33 (31) sts in pattern = 4 in / 10 cm.
Adjust needle size to obtain correct gauge if necessary.

LACE EDGING AND LEG
With 2 strands of Pink held together, CO 72 sts. Divide sts evenly over 4 dpn. Join, being careful not to twist cast-on row; pm for beginning of rnd. Knit 1 rnd.

Lace Edging:
Rnd 1: *K2tog, k3, yo, k1, yo, k3, k2tog tbl, p1*; rep * to * around.
Rnd 2: *K11, p1*; rep * to * around.
Rnd 3: K2tog, k2tog, yo, k1, yo, k1, yo, k1, yo, k2tog tbl, k2tog tbl, p1*; rep * to * around.
Rnd 4: *K11, p1*; rep * to * around.
Rep Rnds 3-4 a total of 3 times.
Now work pattern in stockinette following chart. The first tier of blocks is worked with Pink and White; the rest of the block tiers are worked with Red and White.

HOURGLASS HEEL
After completing 3 tiers of blocks, work the heel with two strands of Pink held together.

Place the 36 instep sts on a holder, and work the first part of the heel back and forth over the rem 36 sts. Slide all 36 heel sts onto one dpn. Begin 2 blocks to the right of the last st, so the dividing line for the sock is in the center of the back, and will then be centered on the sole.

Row 1: Knit across; turn.
Row 2: Begin row with yo, sl 1 (yo + sl 1 = DS), purl to end of row; turn.
Row 3: Yo, sl 1, knit to DS; turn.
Row 4: Yo, sl 1, purl to DS; turn.
Rep Rows 3-4 until there are 12 DS on each side and 12 single sts in the middle.
Knit all around the sock (including instep sts on hold) 2 times. Join each DS (yo + slipped st) as 1 st. Place the 36 instep sts on hold again while you complete the heel.
Row 1: Knit the 12 sts at center of heel + k1; turn.
Row 2: Yo, sl 1, purl the 12 sts at center + p1; turn.
Row 3: Yo, sl 1, k2tog with the k1 + DS, k1; turn.
Row 4: Yo, sl 1, purl to DS, join DS as one st with p2tog, p1; turn.
Rep Rows 3-4 until 36 single sts rem on sole; heel is now complete.

FOOT
With rnd beginning at center of heel, continue working around in stockinette, following chart with Red and White until foot measures 8 in / 20 cm or desired length before toe shaping. Make sure the blocks align.

STAR TOE
Change to two strands of Pink held together. Begin the round at the center of the sole. Knit 1 rnd, *at the same time* decreasing 2 sts evenly spaced around = 70 sts rem.
Rnd 1: (K5, k2tog) around.
Rnds 2-6: Knit.
Rnd 7: (K4, k2tog) around.
Rnds 8-11: Knit.
Rnd 12: (K3, k2tog) around.
Rnds 13-15: Knit
Rnd 16: (K2, k2tog) around.
Rnds 17-18: Knit.
Rnd 19: (K1, k2tog) around.
Rnd 20: Knit.
Rnd 21: (K2tog) around.

Cut yarn and draw end through rem sts; tighten.

FINISHING
Weave in all ends neatly on WS. Make the second sock the same way. See page 22 for instructions on blocking the lace edging so it will be smooth for your finished socks.

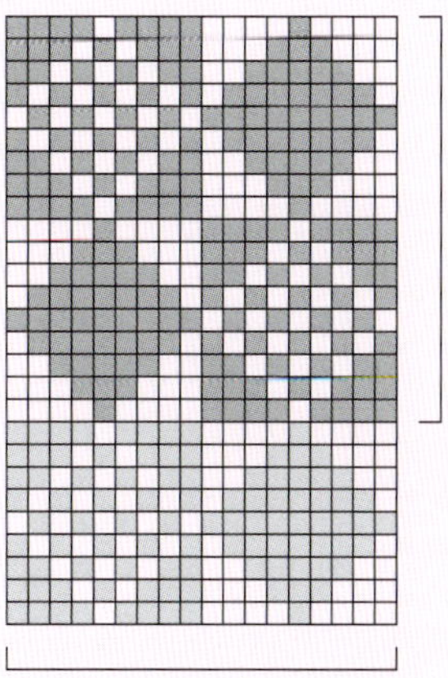

repeat

repeat

☐ Natural
☐ Pink
☐ Red

FOOT

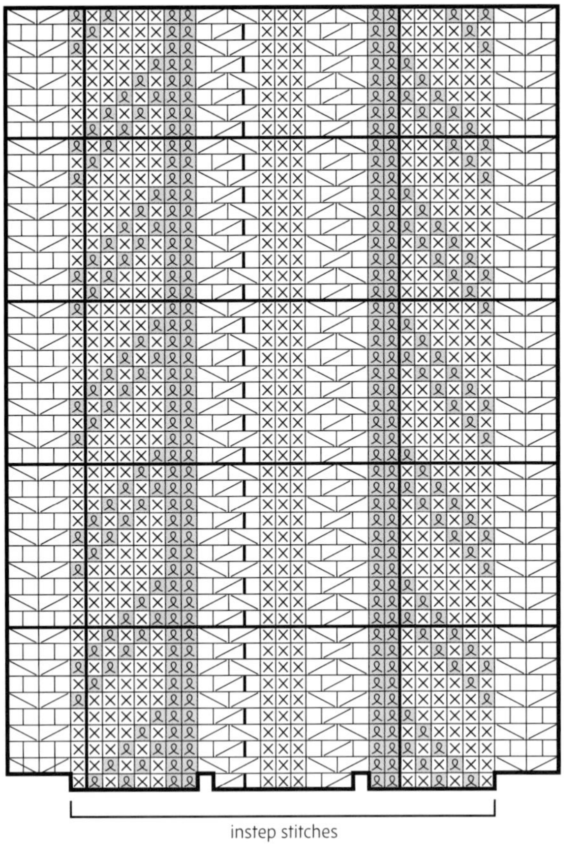

- ☒ purl
- twisted knit (= k1tbl)
- ☐ knit
- Place 1 st on cable needle and hold behind work, k1, k1 from cable needle.
- Place 1 st on cable needle and hold in front of work, k1, k1 from cable needle.

LEG

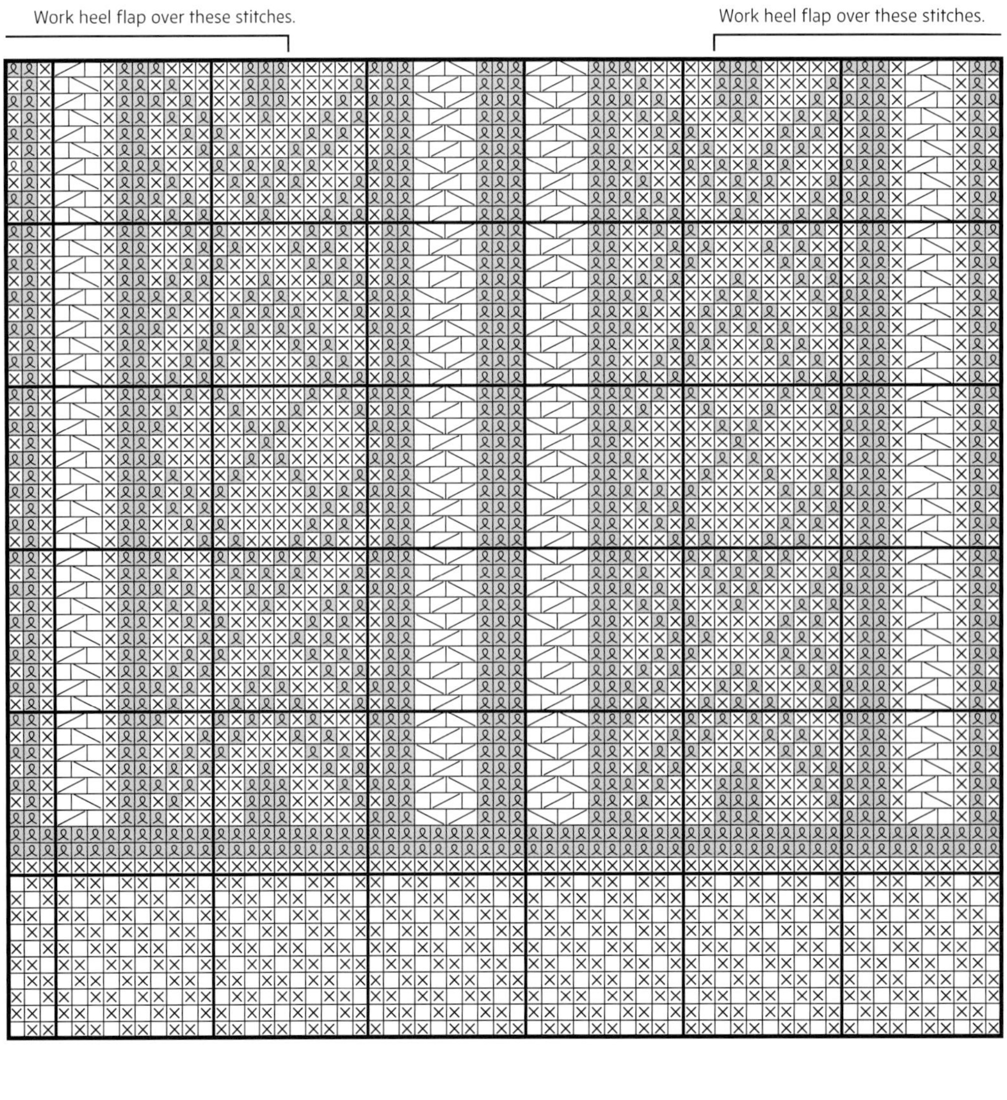

Setesdal *Krot* Socks

Even early in its history in Norway, the technique of knitting was well developed in Setesdal. Everyone recognizes the beautiful lice sweaters from this valley. Stockings, distinctive and typical of the place, were also knitted in Setesdal. The stockings are single-color and the patterns are composed of knit, twisted, and purl stitches together with various cables. All the stockings have sections of cross and crown motifs on the top edging. When these motifs are called "Marius patterns" today, it's only because their origins aren't recognized. These motifs were used in knitting for at least a century before "Marius sweaters" saw the light of day at the beginning of the 1950s.

INSTRUCTIONS
Size: Women's

MATERIALS
Yarn: CYCA #1 (fingering) 2-ply Gammelserie from Rauma (100% wool, 175 yd/160 m / 50 g): Natural White 401, 100 g
Reinforcing Thread: Sewing thread, 100% silk from Amann group, 1 spool, 55 yd/50 m
Needles: U. S. size 1.5 / 2.5 mm: set of 5 dpn; cable needle
Gauge: 24 sts in pattern = 4 in / 10 cm. Adjust needle size to obtain correct gauge if necessary.

LEG
CO 63 sts. Divide sts as evenly as possible onto 4 dpn. Join, being careful not to twist cast-on row; pm for beginning of rnd. Work in pattern following the Leg chart.

COMMON HEEL
After completing sock leg, divide the stitches, placing 27 sts on a holder for instep. These sts will "rest" until the heel is finished.

Heel Flap
Divide the rem 36 sts (those marked on the chart) onto two dpn (= 18 sts per dpn) and work back and forth. Begin with the RS facing you.
Row 1 (RS): Sl 1 purlwise wyb, k35.
Row 2: Sl 1 purlwise wyf, p35.
Repeat these 2 rows until there are 12 chain sts at each side of the flap.

Shaping the Heel
Now you will shape the back by decreasing as follows:
Row 1: Sl 1, knit until 5 sts rem on Ndl 1, k2tog, k3. On Ndl 2, k3, ssk, knit to end of needle.
Row 2: Sl 1, purl to end of row.
Row 3: Sl 1, knit until 4 sts rem on Ndl 1, k2tog, k2. On Ndl 2, k2, ssk, knit to end of needle.
Row 4: Sl 1, purl to end of row.
Row 5: Sl 1, knit until 3 sts rem on Ndl 1, k2tog, k1. On Ndl 2, k1, ssk, knit to end of needle.
Row 6: Sl 1, purl to end of row.
Row 7: Sl 1, knit until 2 sts rem on Ndl 1, k2tog. On Ndl 2, ssk, knit to end of needle.
Row 8: Sl 1, purl to end of Ndl 2. Yarn is now at center of heel flap.
Hold the two dpn with RS facing in (so WS faces out on each side). Join the sets of sts with 3-needle BO: K2tog with 1 st from each needle, *k2tog with next st from each needle, pass first st over the second*. Repeat from * to * until 1 st loop rem.

FOOT
Divide the instep sts onto 2 dpn. With RS facing and with Ndl 1, beginning at the center of the sole, knit to flap and then pick up and knit 1 st in each chain st on the side of the flap = total of 16 sts. You can pick up the chain sts through back loops or knit them tbl on the next rnd. Work the instep sts on Ndls 2-3 in pattern following the chart. With Ndl 4, pick up and knit sts on opposite side of heel flap = 59 sts total.

Move the last 4 sts on Ndl 1 to Ndl 2 and the first 4 sts on Ndl 4 to Ndl 3. Work sole sts in stockinette (Ndls 1 and 4) and instep sts (Ndls 2 and 3) in charted pattern. Work foot to end of foot chart or to desired length before toe.

STAR TOE
Begin at the center of the sole.
Rnd 1: (K5, k2tog) around. The 3 sts rem on Ndl 4 will be decreased in subsequent rnds.
Rnds 2-6: Knit.
Rnd 7: (K4, k2tog) around.
Rnds 8-11: Knit.
Rnd 12: (K3, k2tog) around.
Rnds 13-15: Knit
Rnd 16: (K2, k2tog) around.
Rnds 17-18: Knit.
Rnd 19: (K1, k2tog) around.
Rnd 20: Knit.
Rnd 21: (K2tog) around.

FINISHING
Cut yarn and draw end through rem sts; tighten. Weave in all ends neatly on WS. Make the second sock the same way.

Thumb:

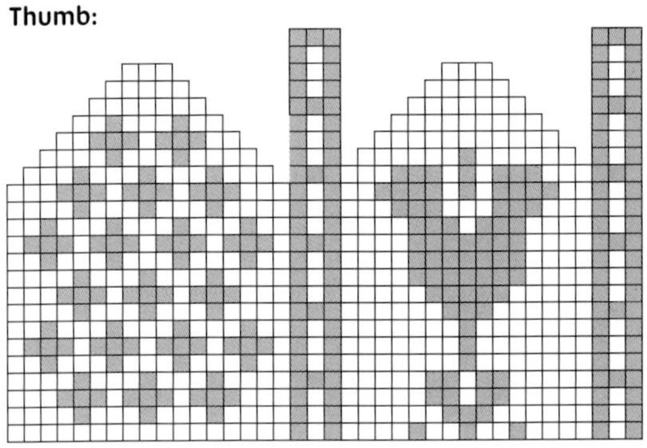

- ☐ White—knit
- ▩ Black—knit
- ▣ Black—purl

CHART 2

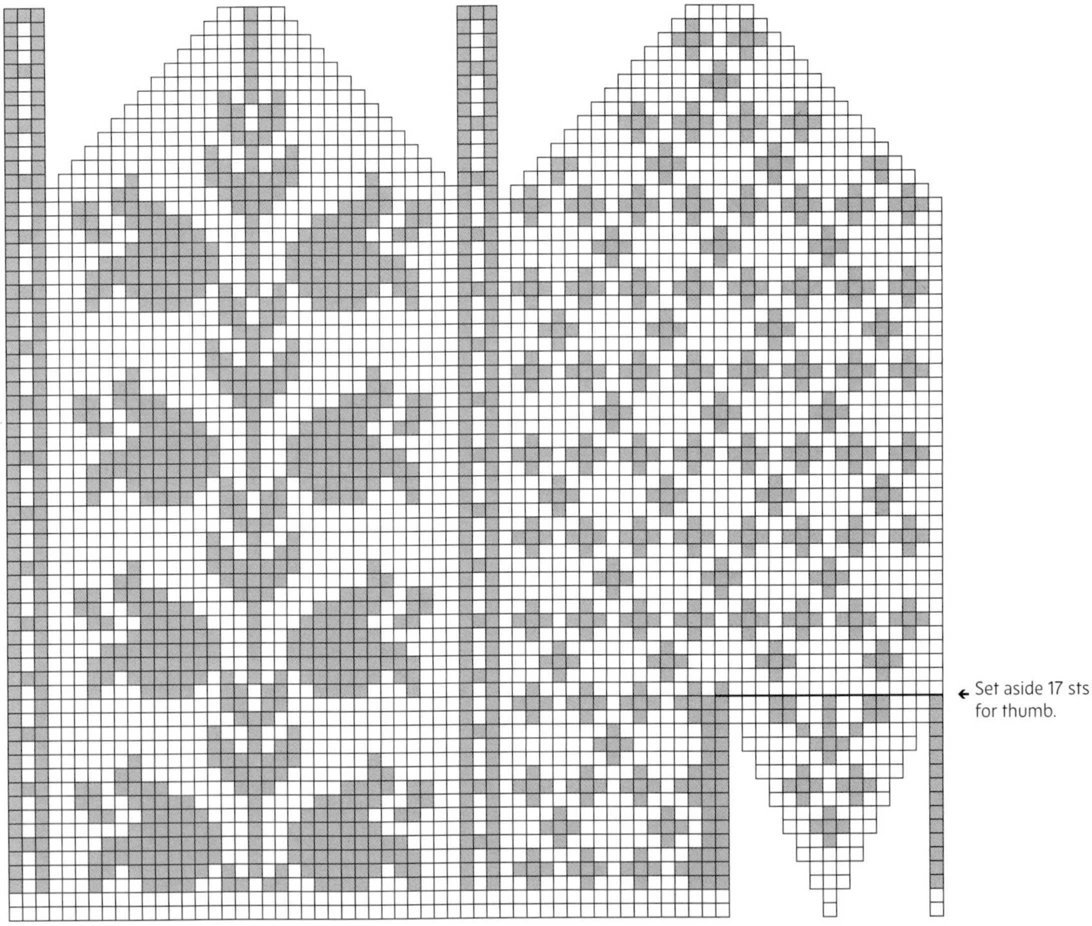

CHART 1

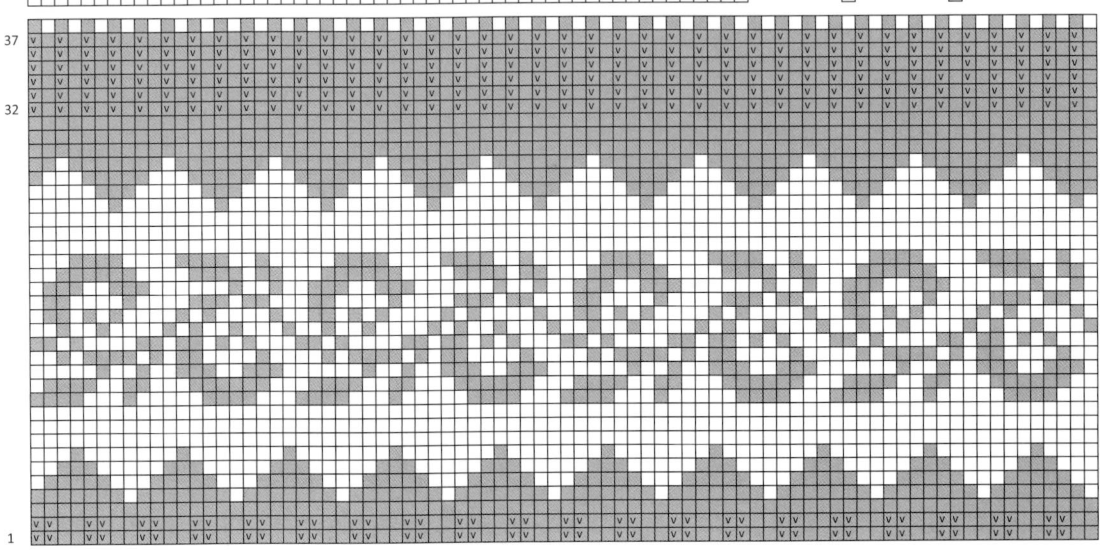

Mittens from Kristiansand

Historically, it was common to leave old and worn textiles at the shoddy mill for recycling and reuse. The materials were shredded and then carded and spun into new yarn, or used as filling for comforters and mattresses. Here, I've reconstructed the pattern on a pair of mittens that were saved at the Torridal Tweed and Wool Comforter Factory in Kristiansand, and which are now in the collection of the West Agder Museum.

INSTRUCTIONS
Sizes: Women's (Men's)

MATERIALS
Yarn:
CYCA #1 (fingering) 2-ply Gammelserie from Rauma (100% wool, 175 yd/160 m / 50 g)
Yarn Amounts
Black 436: 50 (100) g
White 400: 50 (100) g
Needles: U.S. size 0 (1.5) / 2 (2.5) mm, set of 5 dpn
Gauge: 32 (29) sts = 4 in / 10 cm. Adjust needle size to obtain correct gauge if necessary.

Right Mitten
With Black, CO 80 sts. Divide sts over 4 dpn and join to work in the round. Work 2 rnds in k2, p2 ribbing. Continue in St st, following Chart 1 (cuff). On Rnds 32 through 37, work in k1, p1 ribbing as shown.

Continue in St st. On Rnd 39, decrease evenly spaced around to 56 sts. Begin Chart 2, increasing for the thumb gusset as shown. At the dark line, set aside 17 thumb sts for the thumb (see page 15 for details).

Continue, shaping top of mitten as shown on chart (see page 13 for details). Cut yarn and draw end through rem sts; tighten.

THUMB
Pick up and knit 19 + 19 sts around thumbhole = 38 sts total (see page 15). Divide sts onto 4 dpn and work as shown on thumb chart. Cut yarn and draw end through rem sts; tighten.

LEFT MITTEN
Work mirror-image from chart.

FINISHING
Weave in all ends neatly on WS. Gently steam press under a damp pressing cloth to block.

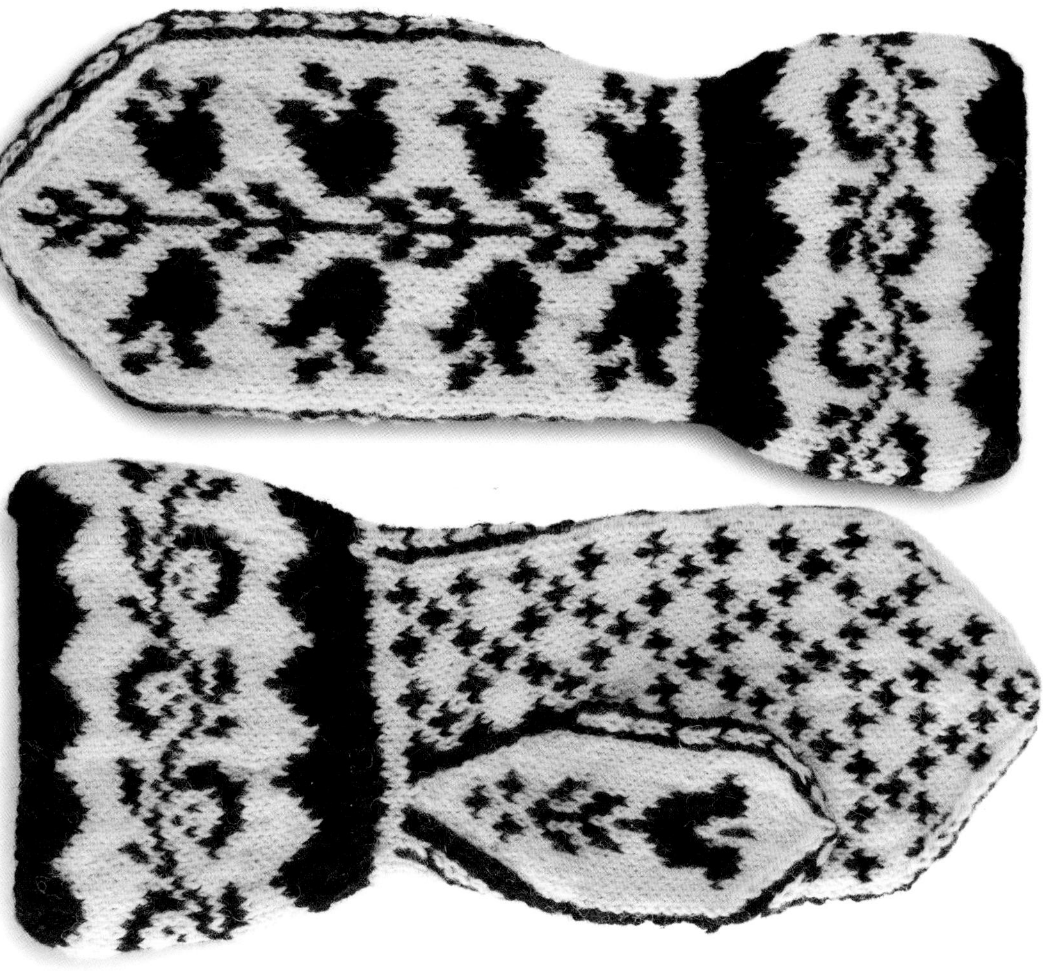

Thumb:

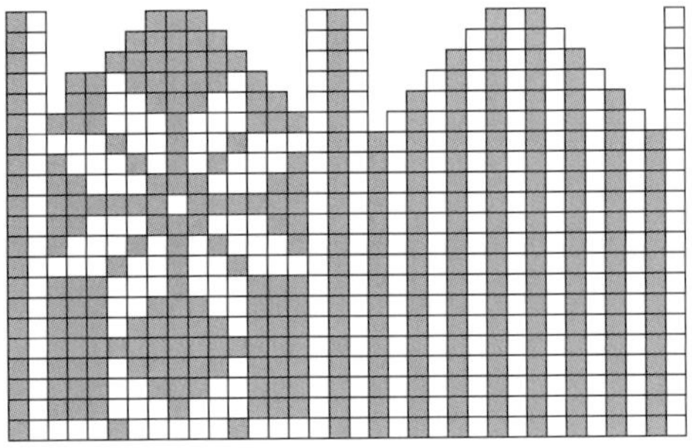

- Gray—knit
- Gray—purl
- Light Blue—knit
- Inc 1 st with Gray.
- Inc 1 st with Light Blue.

Set asic
15 sts f
thumb.

Witchcraft Mittens

Lisbet Pedersdatter is the first Norwegian knitter about whom we have historical records. Lisbet was accused of witchcraft, and her trial was held in Jenns Thommesen's house in Stavanger, on August 22, 1634. From the resulting legal proceedings, we know she made her living knitting stockings. Her name is among a total of 860 people accused of witchcraft in Norway in the 1500s and 1600s; 307 of them were executed, most of them women who were burned alive. I made these mittens to honor all those who were wrongfully accused of witchcraft—hence the name "Witchcraft Mittens."

INSTRUCTIONS
Sizes: Women's (Men's)

MATERIALS
Yarn:
CYCA #1 (fingering) Baby Panda from Rauma (100% Merino wool, 191 yd/175 m / 50 g), Charcoal Gray 14: 50 (100) g
CYCA # (fingering) Cloud from Anzula (hand-dyed 80% Superwash Merino wool, 10% cashmere, 10% nylon, 575 yd/525 m / 100 g), Nimbus Cloud: 50 (100) g
Needles: U.S. size 0 (1.5) / 2 (2.5) mm, set of 5 dpn
Gauge: 40 (36) sts = 4 in / 10 cm. Adjust needle size to obtain correct gauge if necessary.

RIGHT MITTEN
With Charcoal Gray, CO 80 sts. Divide sts over 4 dpn and join to work in the round. Work in k1, p1 ribbing as shown on the chart and then continue in St st.

Increase for the thumb gusset on each side of a center stitch as shown for a striped gusset. At dark line, set aside 15 thumb sts for the thumb (see page 15 for details).

Continue, shaping top of mitten as shown on chart (see page 13 for details). Cut yarn and draw end through rem sts; tighten.

THUMB
Pick up and knit 17 + 17 sts around thumbhole = 34 sts total (see page 15). Divide sts onto 4 dpn and work as shown on thumb chart. Cut yarn and draw end through rem sts; tighten.

LEFT MITTEN
Work mirror-image from chart.

FINISHING
Weave in all ends neatly on WS. Gently steam press under a damp pressing cloth to block.

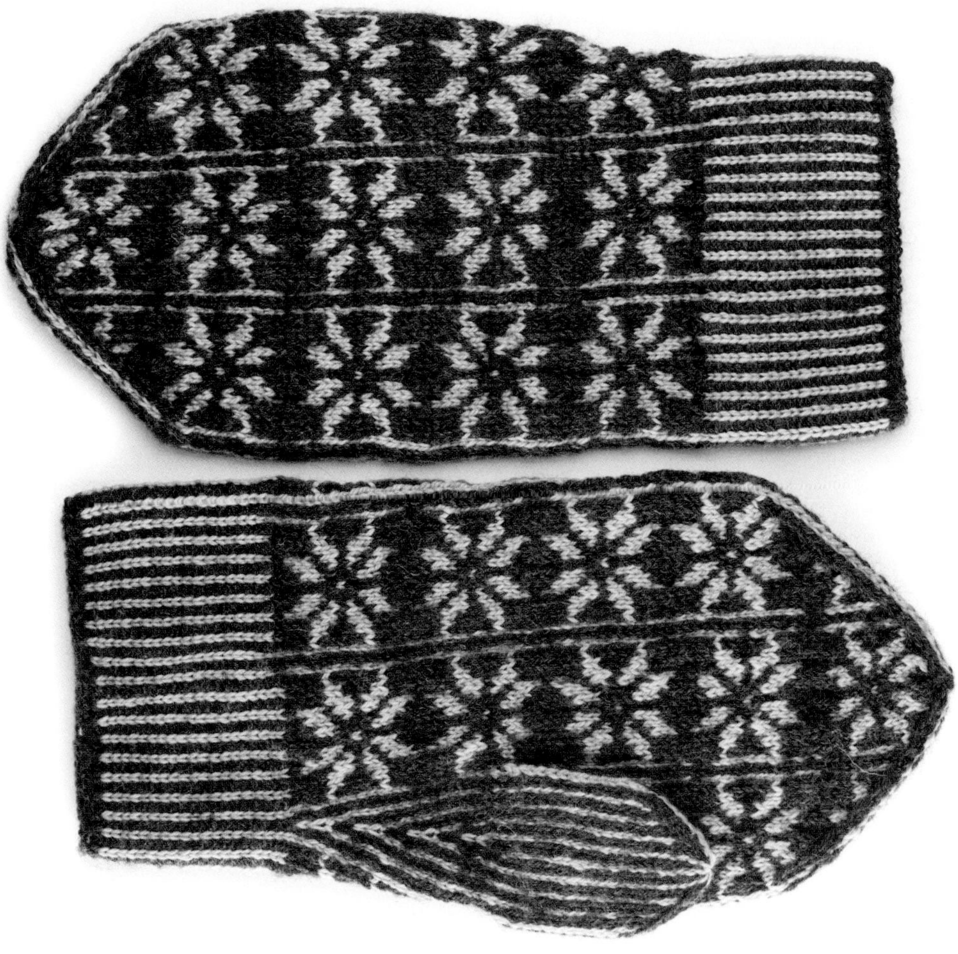

Leftover Party Socks

Until mills began selling machine-spun yarn, people had to use handspun yarn. Spinning was a detailed and time-consuming process. Commercial yarn for knitting wasn't common until a good while later—the early 20th century. The Dale mill was one of the early ones. It produced knitting yarn by 1912, and provided jobs for many women. These days, most of us have yarn leftovers—some have more, some less. There's no reason not to use this extra yarn for smaller projects like socks! We've used 7 colors for these socks. You'll need about 50 grams of the main color, and small amounts of each of the other colors. Just make sure you have enough for both socks.

INSTRUCTIONS
Sizes: Women's (Men's)

MATERIALS
Yarn:
CYCA #1 (fingering) Finullgarn from Rauma (100% wool, 191 yd/175 m / 50 g):
CYCA #1 (fingering) 2-ply Gammelserie from Rauma (100% wool, 175 yd/160 m / 50 g)
Yarn Colors and Amounts:
Finullgarn
Color 1: Green 455: 50 (50) g—you need the most of this color
Color 2: Raspberry Red 456: 50 (50) g
Color 3: Turquoise 4705: 50 (50) g
Color 4: Pink 479: 50 (50) g
Color 5: Yellow 4103: 50 (50) g
Color 6: Orange 4205: 50 (50) g
2-ply Gammelserie
Color 7: Natural White 401: 50 (50) g
Reinforcing Thread:
Mettler extra strong sewing thread, Blue 0350: 33 (66) yd / 30 (60) m
Needles: U. S. size 1.5 (2.5) / 2.5 (3) mm
Gauge: 24 (22) sts in pattern = 4 in / 10 cm.
Adjust needle size to obtain correct gauge if necessary.

LEG
With Raspberry Red, CO 60 sts. Divide sts evenly onto 4 dpn. Join, being careful not to twist cast-on row; pm for beginning of rnd. Work around in k2, p2 rib for 3 rnds.
Next rnd: (K1 Raspberry Rd, k1 Natural) around.
Work purl braid following instructions on page 9; work from X to X.
Now work following Chart 1.
Next rnd: (K1 Raspberry Rd, k1 Natural) around.
Work purl braid following instructions on page 9; work from X to X.
Work following Chart 2.
NOTE: Yellow is knitted on the first rnd and then purled after that.

GUSSET HEEL
After completing the leg, divide the stitches and place the 31 instep stitches onto scrap yarn. These instep stitches will "rest" until the heel is complete. Make sure the pattern is divided symmetrically.

Place the remaining 29 stitches onto one needle and work back and forth with Turquoise and reinforcing thread held together. Begin with the WS facing you.
Row 1 (WS): Sl 1 purlwise wyf, p28.
Row 2: Sl 1 purlwise wyb, k28.
Repeat these 2 rows until there are 14 chain sts at each side of the flap.

Shaping the Heel
Row 1: Sl 1, purl until 10 sts rem on the needle, p2tog, p1; turn.
Row 2: Sl 1, knit until 10 sts rem on needle, ssk, k1; turn.
Row 3: Sl 1, purl until 1 st before gap, p2tog, p1; turn.
Row 4: Sl 1, knit until 1 st rem before gap, ssk, k1; turn.
Repeat Rows 3-4 until all the side sts have been eliminated.
Cut reinforcing thread.

Gusset Shaping
Divide the instep sts from the holder onto 2 dpn; divide the sole sts onto 2 dpn with half of the sts on each. With RS facing, begin working in the round. Begin rnd at center of sole with Green. With Ndl 1, knit to flap; pick up and knit 1 st in each chain up side of flap. You can pick up the chain sts through back loops, or knit them through back loops on the next rnd. With Ndls 2-3, knit across the instep. Next, with Ndl 4, pick up and knit sts down opposite side of flap as for the first side. Knit to center of sole.

On the next rnd, begin decreasing to shape gusset: Knit until 2 sts rem on Ndl 1, k2tog. Knit across instep sts on Ndls 2-3. With Ndl 4, ssk and then knit to end of rnd.
Work the next rnd without decreasing.
Repeat these 2 rnds until 60 sts rem.
Continue without further shaping, with instep and sole in stockinette until foot measures 6¼ (8) in / 16 (20) cm or desired length to toe shaping + Chart 3 rows. Work following Chart 3 and then begin toe shaping.

CHART 1

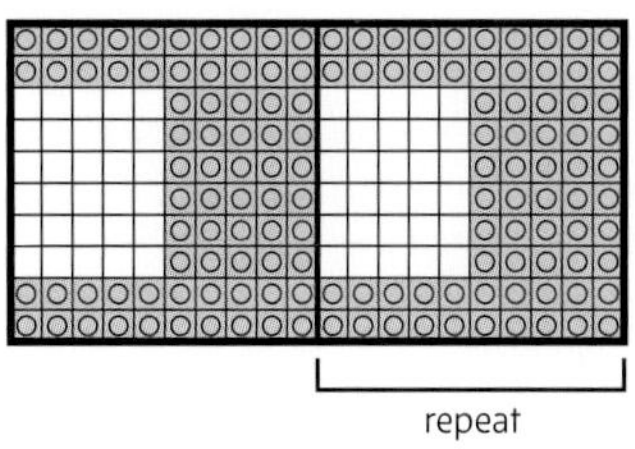

CHART 2

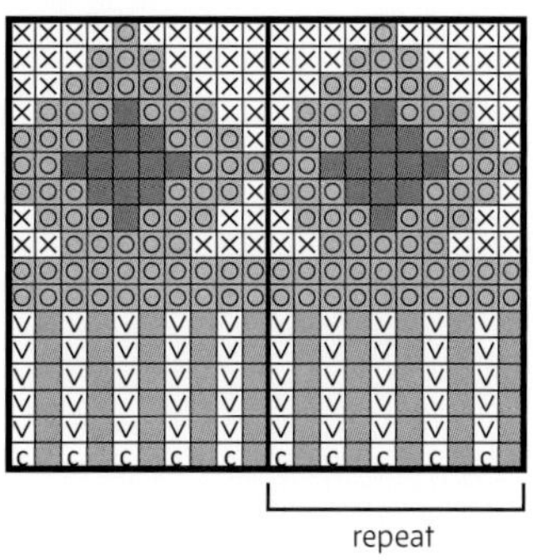

CHART 3

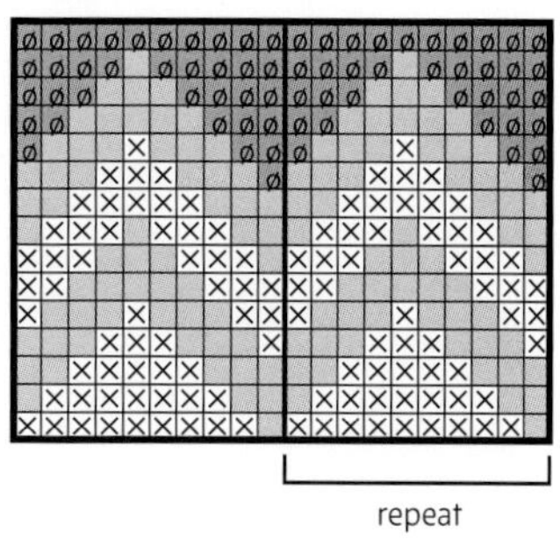

- ☒ Color 1 (Green)—knit
- Color 2 (Raspberry Red)—knit
- Color 3 (Turquoise)—knit
- Color 4 (Pink)—knit
- Color 5 (Yellow—knit
- Color 5 (Yellow)—purl
- Color 6 (Orange)—knit
- ☐ Color 7 (Natural White)—knit

STAR TOE

Begin at the center of the sole with Turquoise.

Rnd 1: (K5, k2tog) around. The 4 sts rem on Ndl 4 will be decreased in subsequent rnds.

Rnds 2-6: Knit.

Rnd 7: (K4, k2tog) around.

Rnds 8-11: Knit.

Rnd 12: (K3, k2tog) around.

Rnds 13-15: Knit

Rnd 16: (K2, k2tog) around.

Rnds 17-18: Knit.

Rnd 19: (K1, k2tog) around.

Rnd 20: Knit.

Rnd 21: (K2tog) around.

FINISHING

Cut yarn and draw end through rem sts; tighten. Weave in all ends neatly on WS. Make the second sock the same way.

Thumb:

- ☐ Red—knit
- ▩ Pink—knit
- ▣ Pink—purl
- ⧅ Sl 1 st to cable needle and hold behind work, p1, k1 from cable needle.
- ⧄ Sl 1 st to cable needle and hold in front of work, k1, p1 from cable needle.

Chart 2:

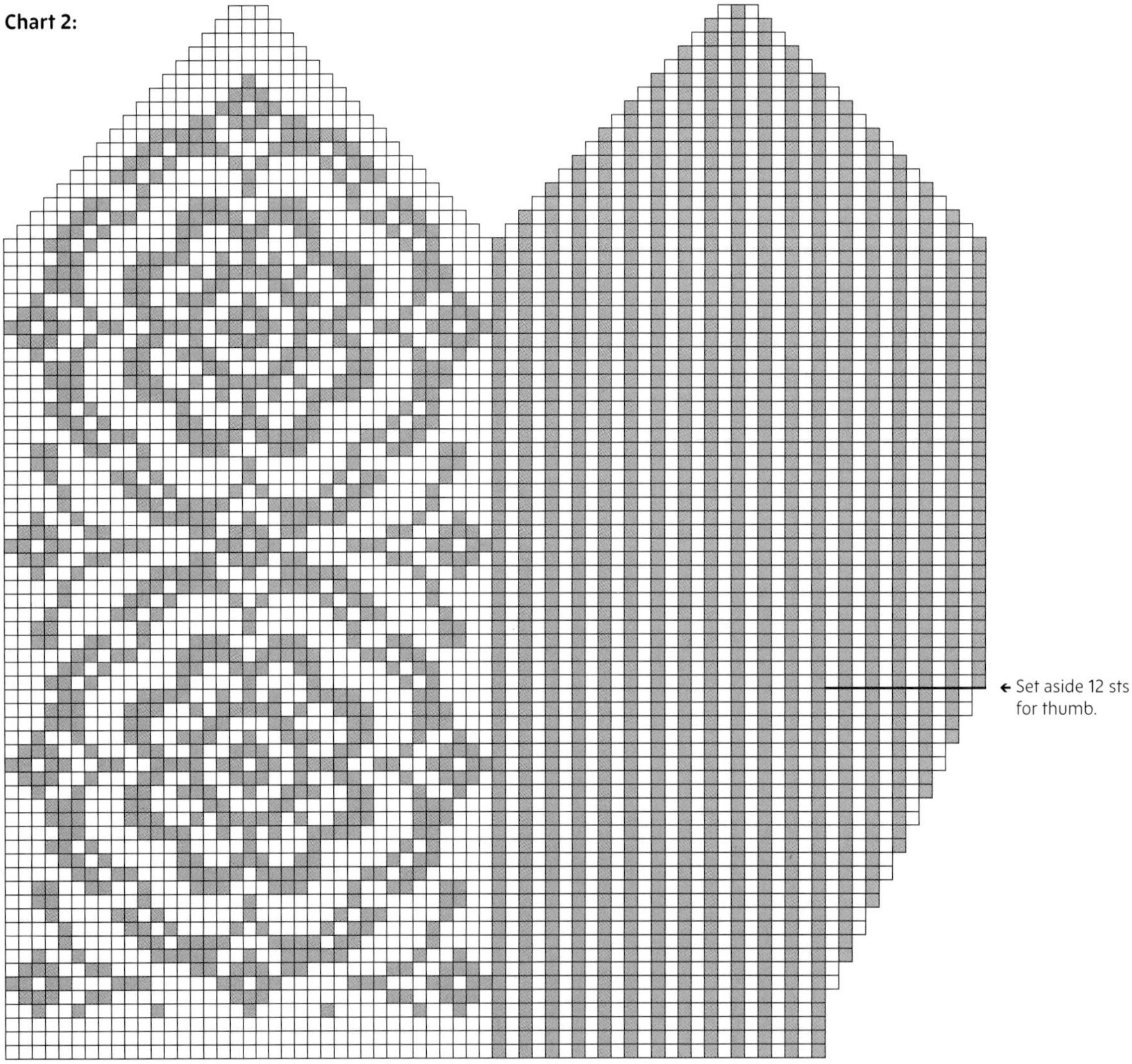

Chart 1:

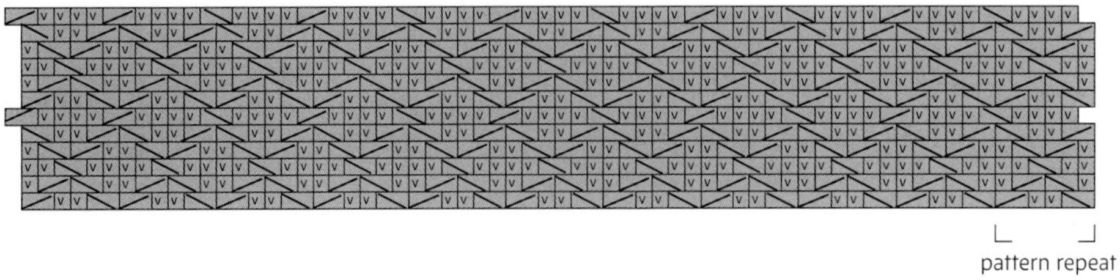

Vestland Rose Mittens

The finer the needles, the more stitches there are across the width of a mitten. With a large number of stitches, the options for patterning increase. For these mittens, I began with a well-known rose pattern, and played a bit with the petal shapes. The result was an entirely new rose. The cuffs on these mittens were inspired by an old pair of mittens from Voss. The technique of crossing stitches used here was well known in Fana, which is just outside Bergen.

INSTRUCTIONS
Sizes: Women's (Men's)

MATERIALS
Yarn:
CYCA #1 (fingering) Dale Babyull from Dale (100% wool, 180 yd/165 m / 50 g)
Yarn Amounts:
Red 4018: 50 (100) g
Embroidery yarn from Setesdal Husflid, Pink: 50 (100) g (or use Dale Babyull, Shocking Pink 4516)
Needles: U.S. size 0 (1.5) / 2 (2.5) mm, set of 5 dpn; cable needle
Gauge: 34 (31) sts = 4 in / 10 cm. Adjust needle size to obtain correct gauge if necessary.

RIGHT MITTEN
With Pink, CO 66 sts. Divide sts over 4 dpn and join to work in the round. Work the cuff following Chart 1. Rep the pattern a total of 4 times in length.

NOTE: The cables are worked from round to round so you will occasionally use sts from the previous and new rnds.

Fold the piece so the right side faces in.

Knit 1 rnd and, *at the same time*, decrease 4 sts evenly spaced around to 62 sts.
Work around in St st with k1 Pink, k1 Red stripes. Continue the stripes until the lining and cuff are the same length—about 4½ in / 11.5 cm. Now continue as shown on Chart 2.

Increase for the thumb gusset as shown. At the dark line, set aside 12 thumb sts for the thumb (see page 15 for details).

Continue, shaping top of mitten as shown on chart (see page 13 for details). Cut yarn and draw end through rem sts; tighten.

THUMB
Pick up and knit 14 + 14 sts around thumbhole = 28 sts total (see page 15). Divide sts onto 4 dpn and work as shown on thumb chart. Shape and finish tip as for top of mitten.

LEFT MITTEN
Work mirror-image from chart.

FINISHING
Weave in all ends neatly on WS. Omitting the cuff, gently steam press under a damp pressing cloth to block. Fold the cuff up.

Stockings from Voss

A pair of confirmation stockings from Voss was among the items registered in connection with Norway's Handcraft Association's exhibit, "Knitting Then and Now," in 1983-84. They were knitted by Maria Olsdatter Årmot (1884-1980) from Myrkjedalen for her daughter Kristi (born in 1909) when she was confirmed. The stockings must have been from the early 1920s. The stockings, which are long and go well over the knees, were dyed after they were knitted. Eventually the feet were re-knitted. Here, I've used the cabled pattern from those stockings on a pair of shorter socks.

INSTRUCTIONS
Sizes: Women's (Men's)

MATERIALS
Yarn:
CYCA #1 (fingering) Sølje from Hillesvåg Ullvarefabrikk (100% Norwegian Pels wool, 383 yd/350 m / 100 g): Lime Green 642107: 100 (150) g
Reinforcing Thread: Mettler extra strong sewing thread in black or similar thread
Needles: U. S. size 1.5 / 2.5 mm: set of 5 dpn; cable needle
Gauge: 26 sts in pattern = 4 in / 10 cm.
Adjust needle size to obtain correct gauge if necessary.

CO 68 (80) sts. Divide sts evenly onto 4 dpn. Join, being careful not to twist cast-on row; pm for beginning of rnd. Work around in k2, p2 ribbing for 10 rnds and, on the last rnd, decrease evenly spaced around to 66 (77) sts. Work the 11-stitch pattern repeat 6 (7) times around. Work the repeat in length 5 times.

GUSSET HEEL
After completing the leg, divide the stitches, placing the 34 (45) instep stitches onto scrap yarn. These instep stitches will "rest" until the heel is complete.

Place the remaining 32 (32) stitches onto one needle and work back and forth with Sølje yarn and reinforcing thread held together. Begin with the WS facing you.
Row 1 (WS): Sl 1 purlwise wyf, p31 (31).
Row 2: Sl 1 purlwise wyb, k31 (31).
Repeat these 2 rows until there are 16 chain sts at each side of the flap.

Shaping the Heel
Row 1: Sl 1, purl until 11 sts rem on the needle, p2tog, p1; turn.
Row 2: Sl 1, knit until 11 sts rem on needle, ssk, k1; turn.
Row 3: Sl 1, purl until 1 st before gap, p2tog, p1; turn.
Row 4: Sl 1, knit until 1 st rem before gap, ssk, k1; turn.
Repeat Rows 3-4 until all the side sts have been eliminated. Cut reinforcing thread.

Gusset Shaping
Divide the instep sts from the holder onto 2 dpn; divide the sole sts onto 2 dpn with half of the sts on each. With RS facing, begin working in the round. Begin rnd at center of sole with Lime Green yarn only. With Ndl 1, knit to flap; pick up and knit 1 st in each chain up side of flap. You can pick up the chain sts through back loops, or knit them through back loops on the next rnd. With Ndls 2-3, work across the instep in pattern as est. Next, with Ndl 4, pick up and knit sts down opposite side of flap as for the first side. Knit to center of sole.

On the next rnd, begin decreasing to shape gusset: Knit until 2 sts rem on Ndl 1, k2tog. Work across instep sts in pattern on Ndls 2-3. With Ndl 4, ssk and then knit to end of rnd.
Work the next rnd without decreasing.
Repeat these 2 rnds until 62 (73) sts rem. Continue without further shaping, with instep in pattern and sole in stockinette, until foot measures approx. 8 (9½) in / 20 (24) cm or desired length to toe shaping. End foot at the end of a complete pattern repeat.

STAR TOE
Begin at the center of the sole.
Rnd 1: (K5, k2tog) around. The 6 (3) sts rem on Ndl 4 will be decreased in subsequent rnds.
Rnds 2-6: Knit.
Rnd 7: (K4, k2tog) around.
Rnds 8-11: Knit.
Rnd 12: (K3, k2tog) around.
Rnds 13-15: Knit
Rnd 16: (K2, k2tog) around.
Rnds 17-18: Knit.
Rnd 19: (K1, k2tog) around.
Rnd 20: Knit.
Rnd 21: (K2tog) around.

FINISHING
Cut yarn and draw end through rem sts; tighten. Weave in all ends neatly on WS. Make the second sock the same way.

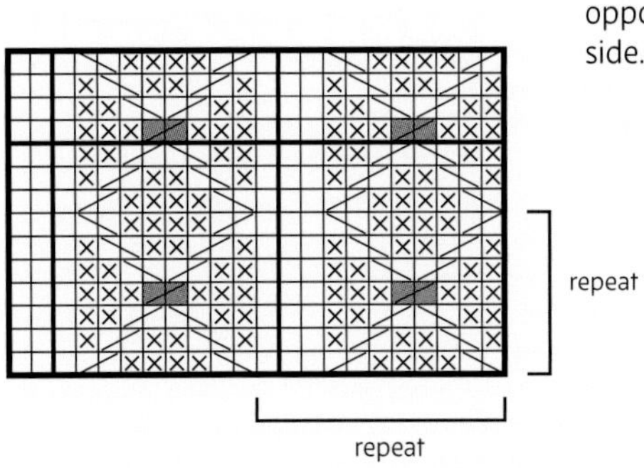

- ☐ knit
- ☒ purl
- Place 1 st on cable needle and hold in front of work, p1, k1 from cable needle.
- Place 1 st on cable needle and hold behind work, k1, p1 from cable needle.
- Place 1 st on cable needle and hold behind work, k1, k1 from cable needle.

CHART 2: INSTEP

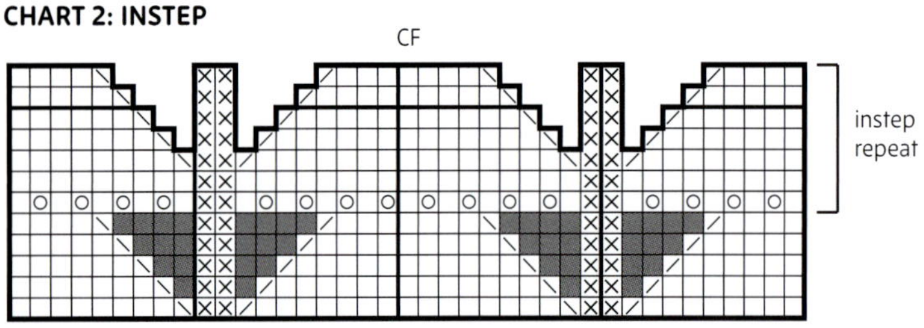

- ☐ knit on RS, purl on WS
- ☒ purl
- ◯ yarnover
- ⏐ Sl 1 wyb without working st.
- ⧅ ssk
- ⧄ k2tog
- ■ no stitch

CF = center front

CHART 1: LEG

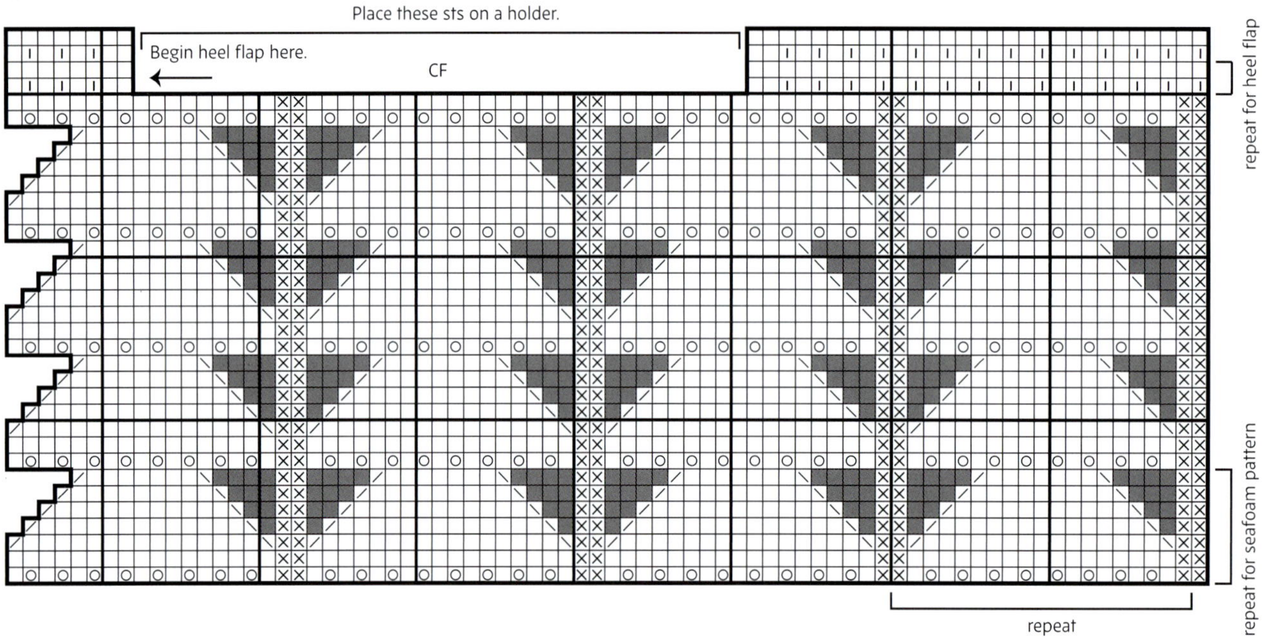

Kroneleistar Socks from Øygarden

The Coast Museum in Øygarden has two pairs of children's socks knitted by Ingrid Mjøs. One pair is slightly larger than the other. Both pairs have "seafoam" patterns, locally referred to as krone patterns—the socks themselves are called *kroneleistar.* These socks were often made as christening socks, because the *krone* pattern symbolized Jesus's crown, which protected the child. The technique is also well known in other countries. Examples of children's socks with similar designs can be found in Stavanger, Herand in Hardanger, and Grong in North Trøndelag, too. It's difficult to say how old this seafoam pattern is, but we find wave patterns in the earliest Scandinavian knitting books, which were published in 1845..

INSTRUCTIONS
Sizes: Women's

MATERIALS
Yarn:
CYCA #1 (fingering) Sheila's Gold from Wool2dye4 (80% Merino Wool, 20% nylon, 400 yd/ 366 m / 100 g)
Yarn Color and Amount:
February Rose hand-dyed by Kate Fredriksen: 100 g
Needles: U. S. size 0 / 2 mm: set of 5 dpn
Gauge: 30 sts in pattern = 4 in / 10 cm.
Adjust needle size to obtain correct gauge if necessary.

LEG
CO 72 sts. Divide sts evenly onto 4 dpn. Join, being careful not to twist cast-on row; pm for beginning of rnd. Work around in k1, p1 ribbing for 8 rnds. Knit the next rnd, decreasing evenly spaced around to 44 sts. Now work seafoam pattern, following Chart 1. **NOTE:** Only the women's size is completely charted in pattern. If you want a longer leg for the socks, work the repeat one or several times extra. When the leg is finished, there are 76 sts.

GUSSET HEEL
After completing the leg, divide the stitches, placing the 39 instep stitches onto scrap yarn. These instep stitches will "rest" until the heel is complete.

Place the remaining 37 sts onto one needle and work back and forth. The leg chart shows which sts are worked for the heel flap on the women's size.
NOTE: The center front of the sock is also the center of a repeat.
Begin with the RS facing you.
Row 1 (RS): Sl 1 purlwise wyb, *k1, sl 1*; rep * to * across, ending with k2.
Row 2: Sl 1 purlwise wyf, purl to end of row.
Repeat these 2 rows until there are 15 chain sts at each side of the flap.
End with Row 1.

Shaping the Heel
Row 1 (WS): Sl 1, purl until 12 sts rem on the needle, p2tog, p1; turn.
Row 2: Sl 1, knit until 12 sts rem on needle, ssk, k1; turn.
Row 3: Sl 1, purl until 1 st before gap, p2tog, p1; turn.
Row 4: Sl 1, knit until 1 st rem before gap, ssk, k1; turn.
Repeat Rows 3-4 until all the side sts have been eliminated.

Gusset Shaping
Divide the instep sts from the holder onto 2 dpn; divide the sole sts onto 2 dpn with half of the sts on each. With RS facing, begin working in the round. Begin rnd at center of sole. With Ndl 1, knit to flap; pick up and knit 1 st in each chain up side of flap. You can pick up the chain sts through back loops, or knit them through back loops on the next rnd. With Ndls 2-3, work across the instep in pattern as shown on chart. Next, with Ndl 4, pick up and knit sts down opposite side of flap as for the first side. Knit to center of sole.

On the next rnd, begin decreasing to shape gusset: Knit until 2 sts rem on Ndl 1, k2tog. Work across instep sts on Ndls 2-3 as shown on chart. With Ndl 4, ssk and then knit to end of rnd. Work the next rnd without decreasing. Repeat these 2 rnds until 24 sts total rem on Ndls 1 and 4 = 63 sts total. Continue without further shaping, with instep in pattern and sole in stockinette until foot measures 6 in / 15 cm or desired length to toe shaping. Try to end the foot with a complete pattern repeat.

STAR TOE
Begin at the center of the sole.
Rnd 1: (K5, k2tog) around. Sts rem on Ndl 4 will be decreased in subsequent rnds.
Rnds 2-6: Knit.
Rnd 7: (K4, k2tog) around.
Rnds 8-11: Knit.
Rnd 12: (K3, k2tog) around.
Rnds 13-15: Knit
Rnd 16: (K2, k2tog) around.
Rnds 17-18: Knit.
Rnd 19: (K1, k2tog) around.
Rnd 20: Knit.
Rnd 21: (K2tog) around.

FINISHING
Cut yarn and draw end through rem sts; tighten. Weave in all ends neatly on WS. Make the second sock the same way.

Mittens from Sogn

This mitten was designed by Thora Gjerland, née Meel (1922-2012). She was an heiress from the estate of Meel in Vetlefjorden in Balestrand. She later married and lived in Leikanger. The mittens featured a design she knitted her whole life, for her relatives and in-laws. The mitten hand is narrow, which makes it fit well. She also knitted shorter mittens without stars on the backs of the hands, for children.

INSTRUCTIONS
Sizes: Women's (Men's)

MATERIALS
Yarn:
CYCA #2 (sport) Ask / Hifa 2 from Hillesvåg (100% wool, 345 yd/315 m / 100 g)
Yarn Amounts
Navy Blue: 50 (100) g
Cream: 50 (100) g
Needles: U.S. size 4 (6) / 3.5 (4) mm, set of 5 dpn

Gauge: 24 (22) sts = 4 in / 10 cm. Adjust needle size to obtain correct gauge if necessary.

RIGHT MITTEN
With Blue, CO 40 sts. Divide sts over 4 dpn and join to work in the round. Work following the chart, beginning with k2, p2 ribbing. Continue in St st pattern, following the chart and increasing for the thumb gusset as shown. At the dark line, place 12 thumb sts on a holder. CO 8 sts over the gap. Continue as charted and shape top as shown (see page 13 for details). Cut yarn and draw end through rem sts; tighten.

THUMB
Pick up and knit 13 + 11 sts = 24 sts total around thumbhole. Divide sts onto 4 dpn and work as shown on thumb chart. Cut yarn and draw end through rem sts; tighten.

LEFT MITTEN
Work mirror-image following the chart.

FINISHING
Weave in all ends neatly on WS. Gently steam press under a damp pressing cloth to block.

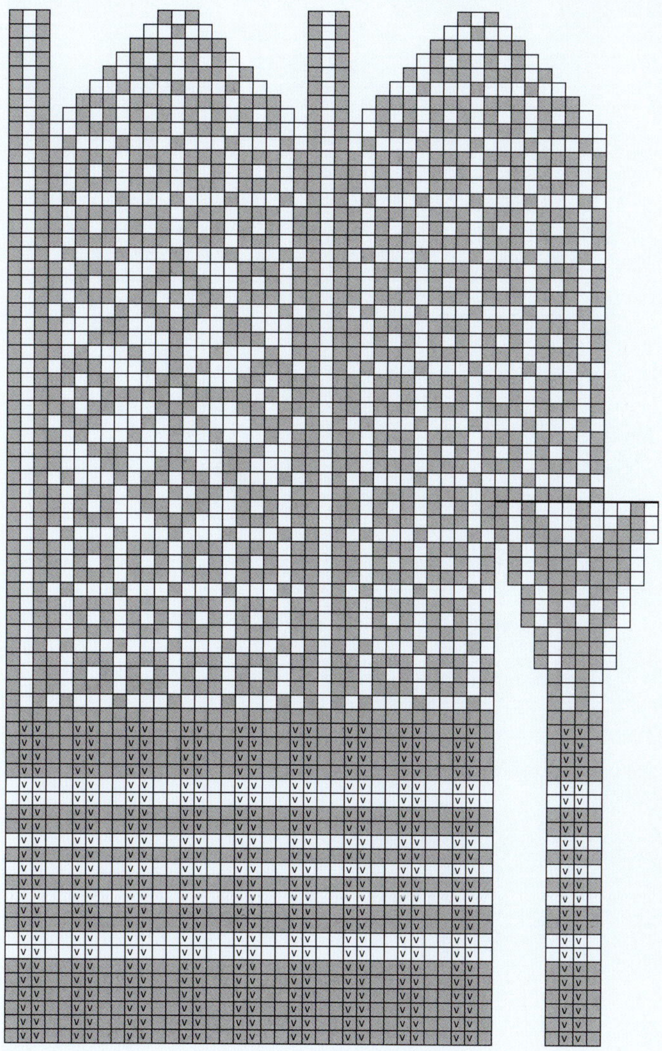

← Set aside 12 sts for thumb.

- ■ Blue—knit
- □ White—knit
- ▣ Blue—purl
- ☑ White—purl

Thumb:

FOOT

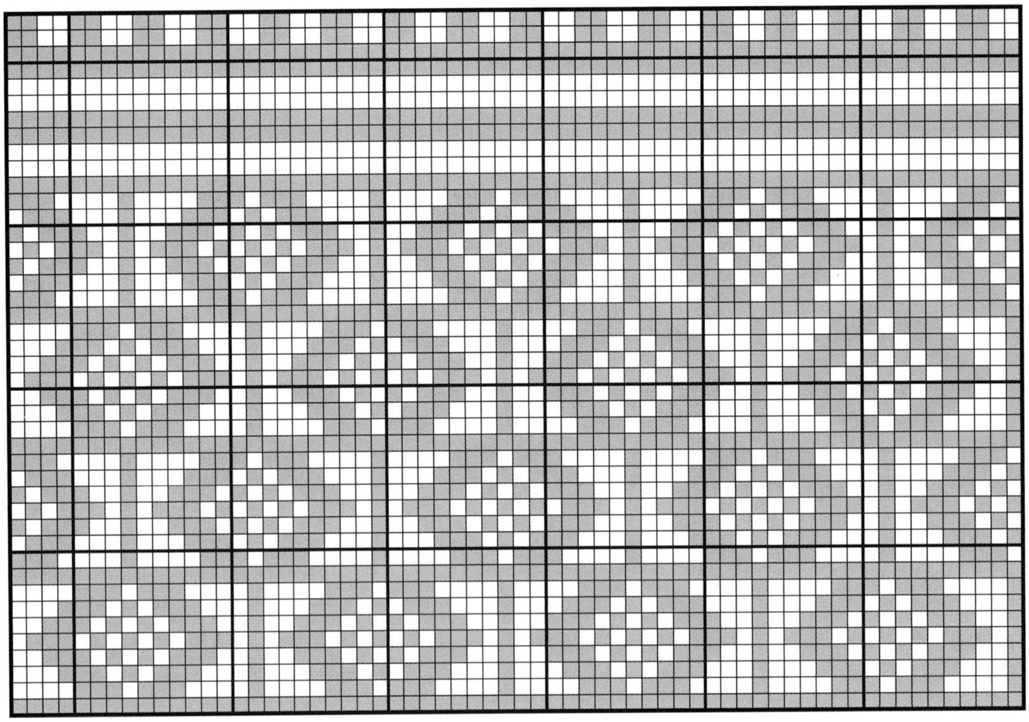

HEEL FLAP

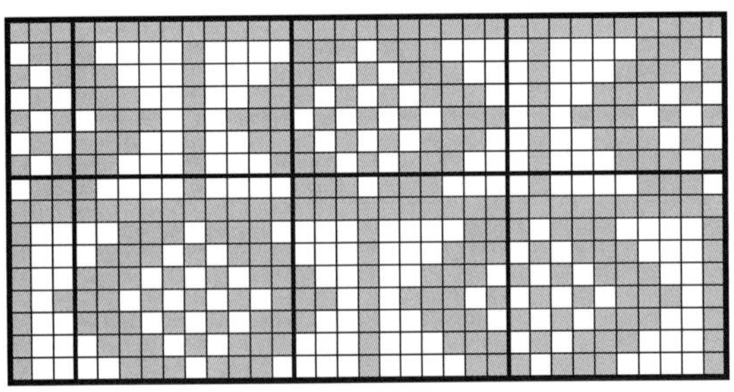

- ☐ Orange—knit on RS and purl on WS
- ▩ Black—knit on RS and purl on WS

LEG

Place these instep stitches on a holder to "rest" while you knit the heel flap.

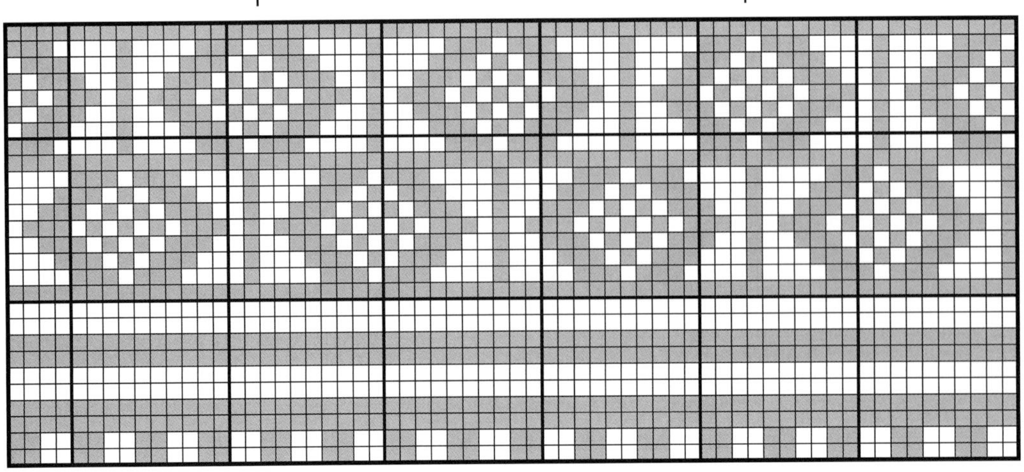

Sunnfjord Socks

Patterns wander. If someone sees a pattern she likes, she'll copy pattern elements. A knitter might add a little panel, a date, or some letters. From Surnadal in Nordmøre and Gaular in Sogn and Fjordane, we see a pattern that's constructed like stones in a wall. The elements of the pattern are arranged in bands; on every other row, the "stones" are shifted so there are no stacked vertical *fuger*, or "joints," as they say in masonry jargon. This pattern appears on mittens in both Surnadal and Gaular, but the University Museum in Bergen also has a pair of stockings with exactly the same pattern. It's a pair from Sunnfjord, knitted in red and black homespun wool yarn.

INSTRUCTIONS
Sizes: Women's (Men's)

MATERIALS
Yarn:
CYCA #1 (fingering), Finullgarn from Rauma (100% wool, 191 yd/175 m / 50 g)
Yarn Colors and Amounts:
Orange 461: 100 (100) g
Black 4387: 50 (50) g
Reinforcing Thread: black silk or similar thread
Needles: U. S. size 1.5 (2.5) / 2.5 (3) mm: set of 5 dpn
Gauge: 30 (28) sts in colorwork pattern = 4 in / 10 cm.
Adjust needle size to obtain correct gauge if necessary.

LEG
With Orange, CO 64 sts. Divide sts evenly onto 4 dpn. Join, being careful not to twist cast-on row; pm for beginning of rnd. Work around in k2, p2 ribbing for 1½ in / 4 cm. Knit 4 rnds in stockinette and then work an eyelet panel as follows: Purl 1 rnd, knit 1 rnd, work eyelet rnd: (k2tog, yo) around, purl 1 rnd.
Continue in stockinette until piece measures 3¼ in / 8 cm long. Now work in leg pattern, as shown on chart.

BAND HEEL
After completing leg, place 31 sts on a holder for the instep (see chart). These sts will "rest" until the heel is finished (see top of leg chart, which indicates instep sts).

Heel Flap
Place the rem 33 sts on one dpn and work the heel flap back and forth. Begin on RS. Work heel flap in pattern as shown on the chart, carrying the reinforcing thread with the black yarn. Work the last st of each row with doubled yarn (1 strand each Orange and Black). Begin on RS as follows:
Row 1 (RS): Sl 1 purlwise wyb, knit to last st, end k1 with both colors.
Row 2: Sl 1 purlwise wyf, purl to last st, end p1 with both colors.
Rep these 2 rows until there are 10 chain sts at each side of flap. Cut black yarn and reinforcing thread; continue with Orange only.

Now decrease to shape the band:
Row 1: Sl 1, knit until 11 sts rem, ssk; turn.
Row 2: Sl 1, purl until 11 sts rem, p2tog; turn.
Row 3: Sl 1, knit until 1 st before gap, ssk; turn.
Row 4: Sl 1, purl until 1 st before gap, p2tog; turn.
Rep Rows 3-4 until all the side sts have been eliminated; cut yarn.

FOOT
Divide the instep sts onto 2 dpn and divide the rem heel sts onto 2 dpn so you have half of each section on a needle. Now work the charted pattern in the round with RS facing you. Begin rnd at center of heel. Pick up and knit 1 st in each chain st along side of heel flap. You can pick up the sts tbl or knit them tbl on next rnd. Work across instep, following chart. Pick up and knit 1 st in each chain st of opposite side of flap and then complete rnd as est = 64 sts total. Continue in foot pattern to end of foot chart. If necessary, you can add a whole or half repeat before the final stripe. Cut Black.

WEDGE TOE
Divide the sts, with 16 sts on each needle
**Ndl 1:* Knit until 3 sts rem on needle, k2tog, k1.
Ndl 2: K1, ssk, knit to end of needle.
Ndl 3: Work as for Ndl 1.
Ndl 4: Work as for Ndl 2.
Knit 2 rnds without decreasing*.
Rep * to * 3 times and then decrease on every other rnd until 3 sts rem on each needle. Cut yarn and draw end through rem sts; tighten.

FINISHING
Weave in all ends neatly on WS. Make the second sock the same way.

Thumb:

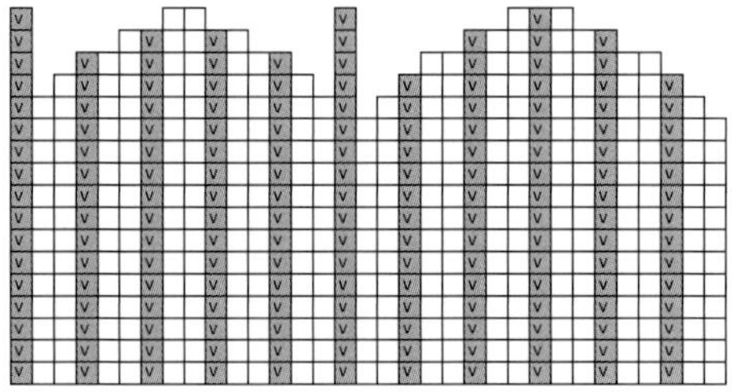

- ☐ Pink—knit
- ▩ Red—knit
- ▣ Red—purl
- ⊡ Inc 1 st knitwise with Pink.
- ⊠ Inc 1 st purlwise with Red.

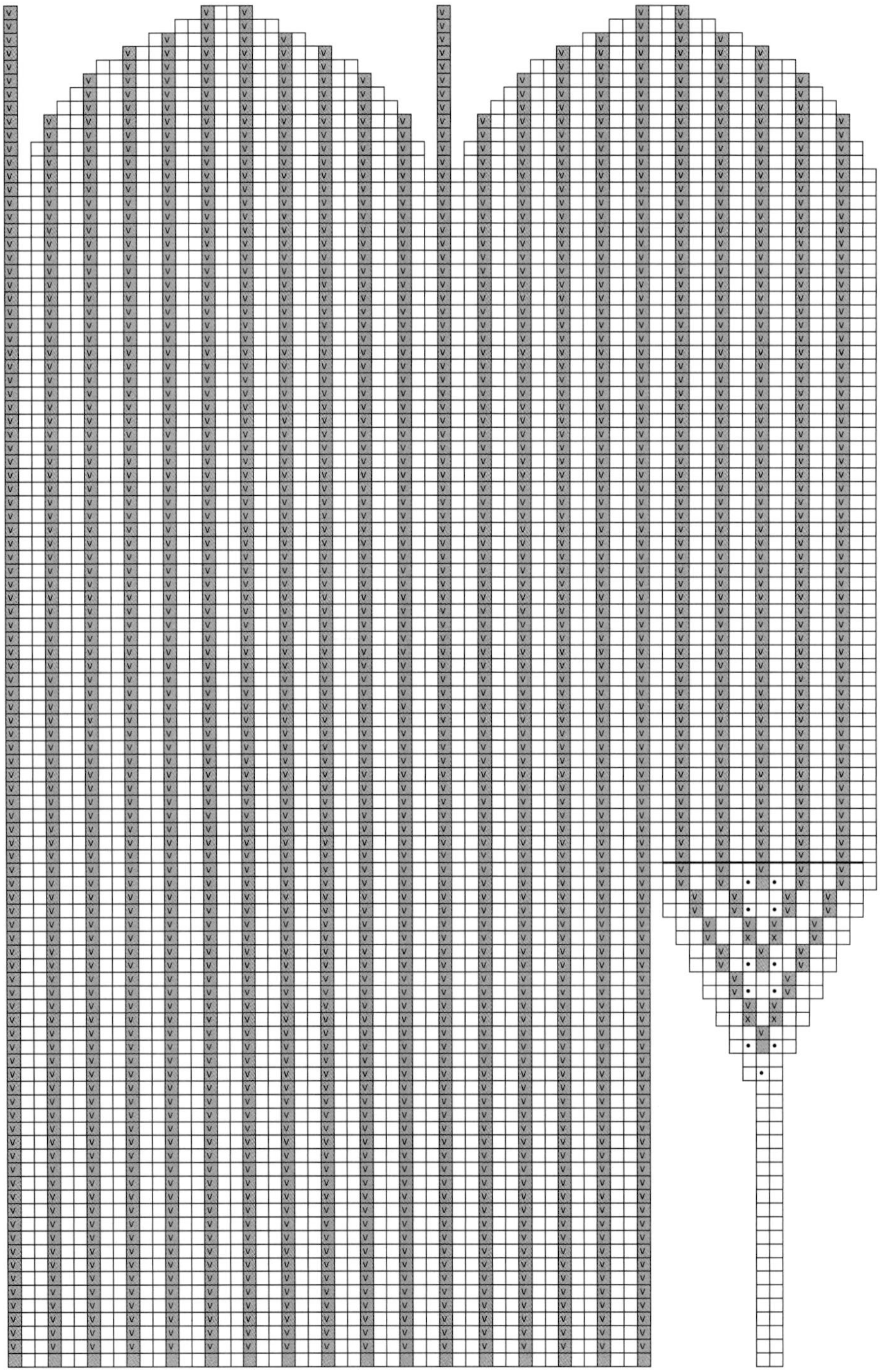

Set aside 15 sts for thumb.

Striped Mittens

I like two-color ribbing, and have experimented with various alternatives. For these mittens, the fine stripes from the beginning continue all the way to the top. The combination of two knit stitches and one purl help make the mittens fit well on the hands.

INSTRUCTIONS
Sizes: Women's (Men's)

MATERIALS
Yarn:
CYCA #1 (fingering) Babyull from Dale (100% Merino wool, 180 yd/165 m / 50 g), Red 4018: 50 (100) g
CYCA #2 (sport) Arroyo from Malabrigo (100% Merino wool, 335 yd/306 m / 100 g), English Rose 057: 50 (100) g
Needles: U.S. size 1.5 (2.5) / 2.5 (3) mm, set of 5 dpn
Gauge: 30 (27) sts = 4 in / 10 cm. Adjust needle size to obtain correct gauge if necessary.

RIGHT MITTEN
With Pink, CO 51 sts. Divide sts over 4 dpn and join to work in the round. Work in St st for ¾ in / 2 cm and then make an eyelet foldline: (k2tog, yo) around. Continue, following the chart.

Increase for the thumb gusset as shown. At the dark line, set aside 15 sts for the thumb (see page 15 for details). Continue following the chart. Shape top as shown on chart (see page 13 for details). Cut yarn and draw end through rem sts; tighten.

THUMB
Pick up and knit 17 + 16 sts = 33 sts total around thumbhole. Divide sts onto 4 dpn and work in pattern as shown on thumb chart. Cut yarn and draw end through rem sts; tighten.

LEFT MITTEN
Work mirror-image following the chart.

FINISHING
Weave in all ends neatly on WS. Fold cuff at eyelet round and loosely sew down edge on WS. Gently steam press under a damp pressing cloth to block.

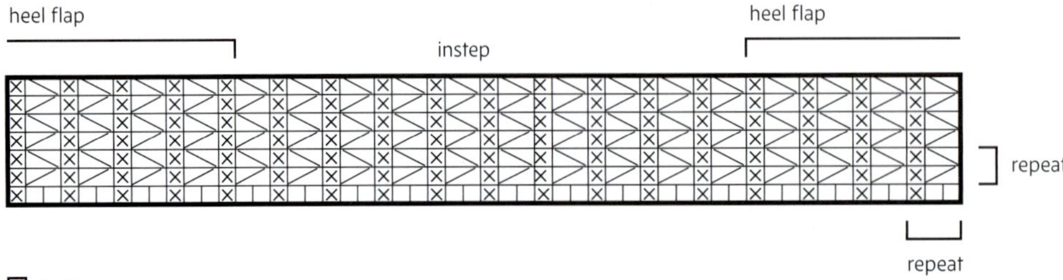

knit

purl

Knit the 2nd st tbl in back of the 1st st without slipping st off needle, knit 1st st, and slip both sts off needle.

Knit the 2nd st in front of the 1st st without slipping it off needle, knit 1st st, and slip both sts off needle.

Zigzag Pattern Socks

Elizabeth I reigned for almost 40 years, and during her reign a number of knitting schools were established in England. The queen would have been attentive to this because at the time, knitting provided a means of income for the poor. It's possible that Denmark's King Christian IV was inspired by the English queen. In Copenhagen, knitting was taught in both orphanages and prisons, which the king had ordered built in the early 1600s. The 1639 charter for a house for women and servants in Trondheim required that they be taught knitting. This is one of the first traces of knitting in Norway. The zigzag pattern in these socks can be found on several pairs of mittens from Jølster.

INSTRUCTIONS

Size: Women's

MATERIALS

Yarn: CYCA #3 (DK, light worsted) Merino DK from Hedgehog Fibres (100% Merino wool, 219 yd/200 m / 115 g)

Yarn Color and Amount:
Seaglass: 100 g

Needles: U. S. size 6 / 4 mm: set of 5 dpn

Gauge: 20 in stockinette = 4 in / 10 cm.
Adjust needle size to obtain correct gauge if necessary.

LEG

CO 54 sts. Divide sts as evenly as possible onto 4 dpn. Join, being careful not to twist cast-on row; pm for beginning of rnd. Begin working in pattern as follows.

Rnd 1: *K2, p1*; rep * to * around.

Rnd 2: * Knit the 2nd st tbl in back of the 1st st without slipping st off needle, knit 1st st and slip both sts off needle, p1*; rep * to * round.

Rnd 3: *Knit the 2nd st in front of the 1st st without slipping it off needle, knit 1st st and slip both sts off needle, p1*; rep * to * around.

Rnds 2-3 form the zigzag pattern. Rep Rnds 2-3 until the leg is 4 in / 10 cm long.

GUSSET HEEL

After completing the leg, divide the stitches, placing the 29 instep sts onto scrap yarn. These instep stitches will "rest" until the heel is complete.

Heel Flap

Place the rem 25 sts (sts indicated on chart) onto one needle and work heel flap back and forth.
Begin with the WS facing you.

Row 1 (WS): Sl 1 purlwise wyf, p24.

Row 2: Sl 1 purlwise wyb, k24.

Repeat these 2 rows until there are 12 chain sts at each side of the flap.

Shaping the Heel

Row 1: Sl 1, purl until 8 sts rem on the needle, p2tog, p1; turn.

Row 2: Sl 1, knit until 8 sts rem on needle, ssk, k1; turn.

Row 3: Sl 1, purl until 1 st before gap, p2tog, p1; turn.

Row 4: Sl 1, knit until 1 st rem before gap, ssk, k1; turn.

Repeat Rows 3-4 until all the side sts have been eliminated.

Gusset Shaping

Divide the instep sts from the holder onto 2 dpn; divide the sole sts onto 2 dpn with half of the sts on each. With RS facing, begin working in the round. Begin rnd at center of sole. With Ndl 1, knit to heel flap. When at side of heel flap, pick up and knit 1 st in each chain up side of flap. You can pick up the chain sts through back loops, or knit them through back loops on the next rnd. Work across instep sts on Ndls 2-3 in pattern. With Ndl 4, pick up and knit sts in each chain st down opposite side of flap as for the first side. Knit to center of sole.

On the next rnd, begin decreasing to shape gusset: Knit until 2 sts rem on Ndl 1, k2tog. Work across instep sts on Ndls 2-3 in pattern. On Ndl 4, ssk and then knit to end of rnd.
Work the next rnd without decreasing.
Repeat these 2 rnds until 54 sts rem.
Continue as est without further shaping until foot measures 8 in / 20 cm or desired length before toe shaping.

WEDGE TOE

Knit the toe entirely in stockinette, decreasing as indicated below. Divide the sts so there are 14 sts on each instep needle and 13 sts on each sole needle. Begin at the center of the sole.

Rnd 1:

Ndl 1: Knit.
Ndl 2: K1, ssk, knit to end of needle.
Ndl 3: Knit until 3 sts rem on needle, k2tog, k1.
Ndl 4: Knit.

Now there are 13 sts on each needle.
Knit 1 rnd without decreasing.
Continue as follows:

Rnd 1:

Ndl 1: Knit until 3 sts rem on needle, k2tog, k1.
Ndl 2: K1, ssk, knit to end of needle.
Ndl 3: Knit until 3 sts rem on needle, k2tog, k1.
Ndl 4: K1, ssk, knit to end of needle.

Rnd 2: Knit without decreasing.

Repeat these two rounds until 3 sts rem on each needle. Arrange the sts with 6 sole sts onto one needle and the 6 instep sts on a second needle. Turn the sock inside out, carefully bringing needles and yarn through. Join the sets of sts with 3-needle BO: K2tog with 1 st from each needle, *k2tog with next st from each needle, pass first st over the second*. Repeat from * to * until 1 st loop rem.

FINISHING

Cut yarn and draw end through rem st loop; tighten. Weave in all ends neatly on WS. Make the second sock the same way.

Thumb:

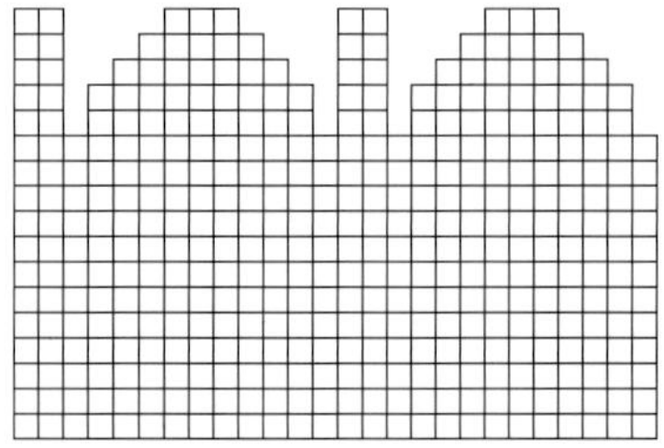

- Pink—knit
- Pink—purl
- Natural White—knit
- Natural White—purl
- Inc 1 st knitwise.

Set aside 11 sts for thumb.

Aasta Mittens

This pair of mittens is named for my good friend Aasta Olstad, who was born in Røtvei in 1928 and grew up on her grandparents' farm in Oppdal. Her grandmother spun yarn and wove fabric. At an early age, Aasta and her sister, Eli, who was a year younger, had to learn to card wool. It was hard work all winter for such small girls. During the summers, they knitted when they were at the summer pasture. Both girls had to make whatever they needed in terms of mittens and socks. To sit without any work in your hands just wasn't allowed. The pattern panels on these cuffs were inspired by the decorative edge of an old glove.

INSTRUCTIONS
Sizes: Women's (Men's)

MATERIALS
Yarn:
CYCA #3 (DK) Sterk from Du Store Alpakka (40% Merino wool, 40% alpaca, 20% polyamide, 150 yd/137 m / 50 g), Natural White 806: 100 (100) g
CYCA #2 (sport) Arroyo from Malabrigo (100% Merino wool, 335 yd/306 m / 100 g), English Rose 057: 50 g
Needles: U.S. size 2.5 (4) / 3 (3.5) mm, set of 5 dpn
Gauge: 25 (22) sts = 4 in / 10 cm. Adjust needle size to obtain correct gauge if necessary.

RIGHT MITTEN
With Pink, CO 56 sts. Divide sts over 4 dpn and join to work in the round. Work around in k2, p2 ribbing as shown on chart. Continue in color pattern and St st following the chart. When the cuff is complete, begin thumb gusset, increasing as shown. The st on each side of the gusset is purled. At the dark line, set aside 11 sts for the thumb (see page 15 for details). Shape top as shown on chart (see page 13 for details). Cut yarn and draw end through rem sts; tighten.

THUMB
Pick up and knit 13 + 13 sts = 26 sts total around thumbhole (see page 15). Divide sts onto 4 dpn and work as shown on thumb chart. Cut yarn and draw end through rem sts; tighten.

LEFT MITTEN
Work mirror-image following the chart.

FINISHING
Weave in all ends neatly on WS. Gently steam press under a damp pressing cloth to block.

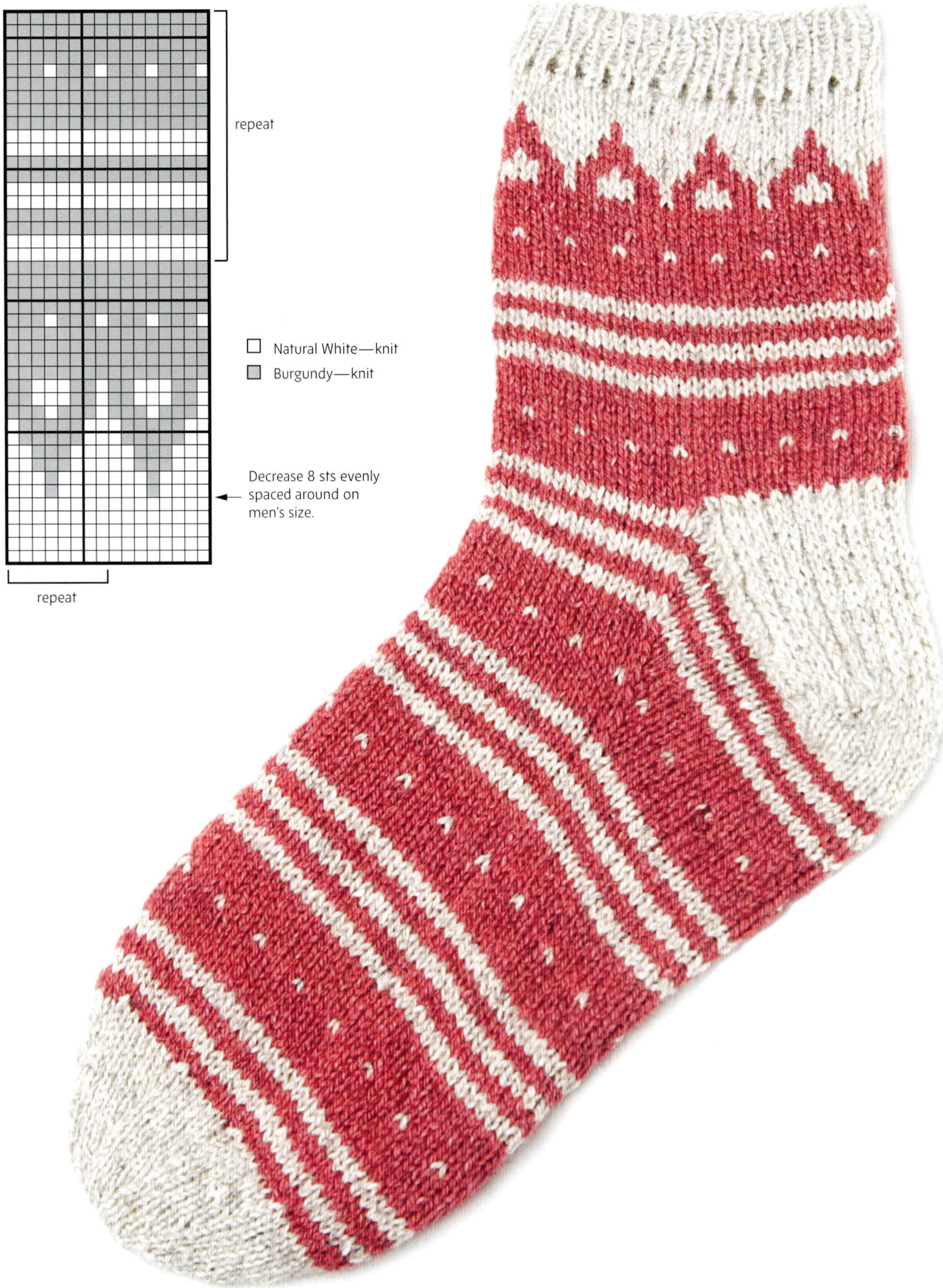
repeat
Natural White—knit
Burgundy—knit
Decrease 8 sts evenly spaced around on men's size.
repeat

Striped Socks from Orkladalen

Stripes are one of the easiest ways to add patterning to knitted items. Horizontal stripes became quite the trend in the second half of the nineteenth century, and a large number of striped socks have survived from that period. All sorts of striping sequences were used, from simple stripes all the same width to a variety of stripe repeats. The starting point for these stockings is a pair from Meldal/Rennebu, registered at The Norwegian Institute for Bunad and Folk Costume on Fagneres, knitted with red and white wool yarn. At the top is a wide section of diagonally striped lace followed by an elegant two-color panel, making the stockings distinctive.

INSTRUCTIONS
Sizes: Women's (Men's)

MATERIALS
Yarn:
CYCA #1 (light fingering) Samite Silk Blend from Blacker Yarns (40% Shetland wool, 30% Bluefaced Leicester wool, 20% Eri silk, 10% Gotland wool, 503 yd/460 m / 100 g)
Yarn Colors and Amounts:
Aspen's Shiver, Natural White: 100 (100) g
Fiery Dew, Burgundy: 100 (100) g
Needles: U. S. size 1.5 / 2.5 mm: set of 5 dpn
Gauge: 24 sts in pattern = 4 in / 10 cm.
Adjust needle size to obtain correct gauge if necessary.

LEG
With Natural White, CO 64 (72) sts. Divide sts evenly onto 4 dpn. Join, being careful not to twist cast-on row; pm for beginning of rnd. Work around in k1, p1 ribbing for 10 rnds. Now work an eyelet rnd: K1, (yo, k2tog) around. End by slipping the 1st st (the single knit st) to Nsdl 4, yo, k2tog.
Next, work in pattern following the chart. On the men's size, decrease 8 sts evenly spaced around on the last rnd [= (k7, k2tog) around = 64 sts rem] before beginning with the Burgundy yarn.

GUSSET HEEL
After completing the leg, divide the stitches in half, placing the 32 (32) instep stitches onto scrap yarn. These instep stitches will "rest" until the heel is complete.

Place the remaining 32 (32) sts onto one needle and work back and forth. Work heel flap with Natural White only. Begin with the WS facing you, work the reinforced heel pattern.
Row 1 (WS): Sl 1 purlwise wyf, purl to end of row.
Row 2: Sl 1 purlwise wyb, (k1, sl 1) to last st; end k1.
Repeat these 2 rows until there are 15 (16) chain sts at each side of the flap.

Shaping the Heel
Row 1 (WS): Sl 1, purl until 11 sts rem on the needle, p2tog, p1; turn.
Row 2: Sl 1, knit until 11 sts rem on needle, ssk, k1; turn.
Row 3: Sl 1, purl until 1 st before gap, p2tog, p1; turn.
Row 4: Sl 1, knit until 1 st rem before gap, ssk, k1; turn.
Repeat Rows 3-4 until all the side sts have been eliminated.

Gusset Shaping
Divide the instep sts from the holder onto 2 dpn; divide the sole sts onto 2 dpn with half of the sts on each. With RS facing and Natural White, begin working in the round. Begin rnd at center of sole. With Ndl 1, knit to flap; pick up and knit 1 st in each chain up side of flap. You can pick up the chain sts through back loops, or knit them through back loops on the next rnd. With Ndls 2-3, knit across the instep. Next, with Ndl 4, pick up and knit sts down opposite side of flap as for the first side. Knit to center of sole.

On the next rnd, begin decreasing to shape gusset: Knit until 2 sts rem on Ndl 1, k2tog. Knit across instep sts on Ndls 2-3. With Ndl 4, ssk and then knit to end of rnd.
Attach Burgundy and work the next rnd in charted pattern without decreasing.
Repeat these 2 rnds, working in charted pattern, until 58 (64) sts rem.

Continue in pattern without further shaping until foot measures approx. 7 (9½) in / 18 (24) cm or desired length to toe shaping. Decrease 2 (1) sts before you begin the last stripe = 56 (63) sts rem.

STAR TOE
Begin at the center of the sole with Natural White.
Rnd 1: (K5, k2tog) around.
Rnds 2-6: Knit.
Rnd 7: (K4, k2tog) around.
Rnds 8-11: Knit.
Rnd 12: (K3, k2tog) around.
Rnds 13-15: Knit
Rnd 16: (K2, k2tog) around.
Rnds 17-18: Knit.
Rnd 19: (K1, k2tog) around.
Rnd 20: Knit.
Rnd 21: (K2tog) around.

FINISHING
Cut yarn and draw end through rem sts; tighten. Weave in all ends neatly on WS. Make the second sock the same way.

Ragg Socks from Hitra

The Coast Museum in South Trøndelag has a pair of relatively coarse gray wool socks in their collection. The feet are knitted in stockinette, and the rest of each sock is worked in ribbing. We can find socks of this type all around the country. They were warm, everyday socks without any unnecessary ornamentation. The embroidery was only to indicate whose socks they were, not for embellishment. The ribbing meant the socks fit the feet especially well. Certainly along the coast, it was important to have sturdy socks. When out cod fishing for several months, it was typical to have several pairs stowed away in the equipment chest.

INSTRUCTIONS
Sizes: Women's (Men's)

MATERIALS
Yarn:
CYCA #2 (sport, baby) 3-ply Sand Spelsau yarn from Lofoten Wool (100% Spelsau wool, 230 yd/210 m / 100 g)
Yarn Color and Amount:
Sand: 150 (150) g
Needles:
U. S. size 4 / 3.5 mm: set of 5 dpn
Gauge: 17 sts in pattern = 4 in / 10 cm. Adjust needle size to obtain correct gauge if necessary.

LEG
CO 48 (52) sts. Divide sts evenly onto 4 dpn. Join, being careful not to twist cast-on row; pm for beginning of rnd. Work around in k2, p2 ribbing for 5½ in / 14 cm.

BAND HEEL WITH SHORT HEEL FLAP
After completing leg, place 26 (30) sts on a holder for the instep (to "rest" while you work the heel flap).

Heel Flap
Place rem 22 sts on one dpn and work heel flap back and forth.
Begin with WS facing you.
Row 1 (WS): Sl 1 purlwise wyf, purl to end of row.
Row 2: Sl 1 purlwise wyb, knit to end of row.
Rep these 2 rows until there are 8 chain sts at each side of flap.

Heel Gusset:
Row 1: Sl 1, purl until 8 sts rem, p2tog; turn.
Row 2: Sl 1, knit until 8 sts rem, ssk; turn.
Row 3: Sl 1, purl until 1 st before gap, p2tog; turn.
Row 4: Sl 1, knit until 1 st before gap, ssk; turn.
Rep Rows 3-4 until all the side sts have been eliminated.

FOOT
Divide the instep sts onto 2 dpn and divide the rem heel sts onto 2 dpn so you have half of each section on a needle. Work in the round with RS facing you. Begin rnd at center of sole. Knit to heel flap. Pick up and knit 1 st in each chain st along side of heel flap. You can pick up the sts tbl or knit them tbl on next rnd. Work in ribbing as est across instep. Pick up and knit sts in chain sts of opposite side of flap and then knit to end of rnd = 50 (54) sts.

Begin at the center of the sole. K2, k2tog, k8, work 26 (30) sts in ribbing, k8, ssk, k2 = 48 (52) sts rem.
Now work foot with ribbing across instep and stockinette on sole until sock measures 9 (9) in / 20 (23) cm or desired length to toe shaping.

WEDGE TOE
Divide the sts evenly onto 4 dpn.
**Ndl 1:* Knit until 3 sts rem on needle, k2tog, k1.
Ndl 2: K1, ssk, work ribbing to end of needle.
Ndl 3: Work ribbing to last 3 sts and end with k2tog, k1.
Ndl 4: K1, ssk, knit to end of needle.
Knit 1 rnd without decreasing*.
Rep * to * 3 times and then decrease on every rnd until 4 sts rem on each needle. Cut yarn and draw end through rem sts; tighten.

FINISHING
Weave in all ends neatly on WS. Make the second sock the same way.

- Light Gray—knit
- Dark Gray—knit
- Dark Gray—purl
- Inc 1 st with Light Gray.
- Inc 1 st with Dark Gray.
- no stitch
- k2tog tbl with Light Gray
- k2tog tbl with Dark Gray
- k2tog tbl with Dark Gray
- k2tog tbl with Light Gray
- k2tog with Light Gray
- k2tog with Dark Gray
- k2tog with Dark Gray
- k2tog with Light Gray

Thumb:

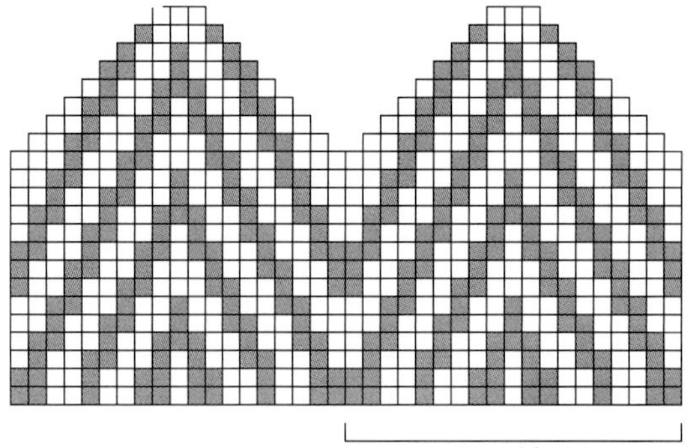

Chart 2:

Chart 1:

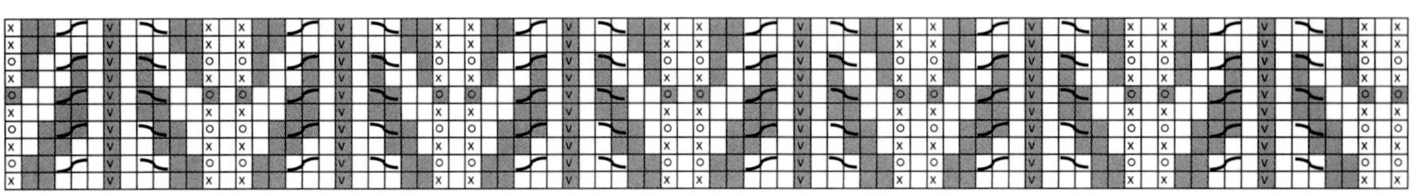

Mittens from Gauldal

Here, I've reconstructed a pair of mittens registered during the fieldwork undertaken by the Norwegian Folk Museum in Budalen in Midtre Gauldal in 1987. The pattern consists of simple diamond blocks in black and gray covering the entire mitten. There is a cross inside each block, and the thumb was knitted in a typical fishbone pattern.

INSTRUCTIONS
Sizes: Women's (Men's)

MATERIALS
Yarn:
CYCA #2 (sport) Mohair by Canard (65% mohair, 35% Merino wool, 193 yd/176 m / 50 g)
Yarn Amounts:
Dark Gray 2101: 50 (100) g
Light Gray 2102: 50 (100) g
Needles: U.S. size 1.5 (2.5) / 2.5 (3) mm, set of 5 dpn
Gauge: 31 (28) sts = 4 in / 10 cm. Adjust needle size to obtain correct gauge if necessary.

RIGHT MITTEN
With Dark Gray, CO 56 sts. Divide sts over 4 dpn and join to work in the round. Work 6 rnds in St st and then continue in pattern on Chart 2. Increase for thumb gusset as shown, increasing on each side of a center st. At the dark line, set aside 17 sts for the thumb (see page 15 for details). Continue following the chart. Shape top as shown on chart (see page 13 for details on shaping). Cut yarn and draw end through rem sts; tighten.

THUMB
Pick up and knit 19 + 19 sts = 38 sts total around thumbhole. Divide sts onto 4 dpn and work in pattern as shown on thumb chart. Cut yarn and draw end through rem sts; tighten.

CUFF
With Light Gray, CO 72 sts. Divide sts over 4 dpn and join to work in the round. Work in pattern as shown on Chart 1. After completing the last rnd, 60 sts rem. Dec another 4 sts evenly spaced around = 56 sts rem.

Joining Mitten and Cuff
Pick up and knit 56 sts around edge of mitten and divide sts onto 4 dpn with 14 sts on each needle. Divide the sts on the cuff so there are also 14 sts on each of the 4 dpn. Place the cuff outside the mitten. Make sure that the center of the repeat is aligned with the center of the mitten. Join the cuff and mitten by working three-needle bind-off around.
Three-needle bind-off: K2tog (with 1 st from each needle), *k2tog; pass 1st st on right needle over 2nd; rep from * until all sts have been bound off.

LEFT MITTEN
Work mirror-image following the chart.

FINISHING
Weave in all ends neatly on WS. Pin out mittens, pinning out cuffs so that gentle waves follow the pattern. Sprinkle well with water and leave to dry for at least 24 hours.

Thumb:

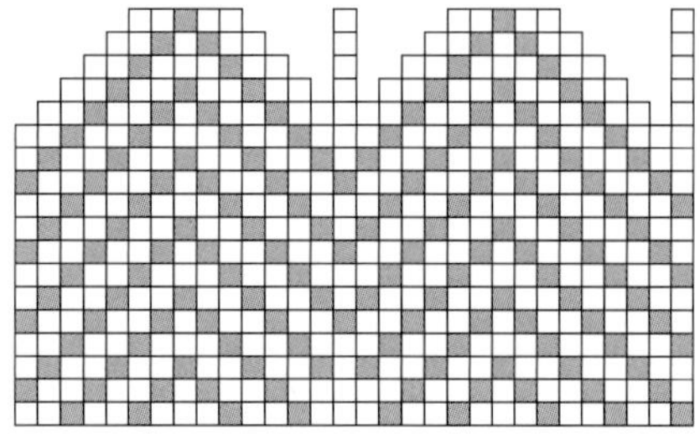

☐ Red-Violet—knit
■ Light Gray—knit

← Set aside 13 sts for thumb.

Krus Mittens from Røros

These mittens are what Norwegians call *krus* mittens; the pattern is based on a pair from Mikkelssgården at Feragen, where the owner lived between 1851 and 1947. The original mittens were knitted with red and black yarn, and the pattern consisted of eight-petaled roses placed closely together. That pair, which must have been knitted with exceptionally fine yarn, had five pattern repeats on each side, which adds up to 112 stitches around. The exact same pattern can be seen on a pair of wrist warmers from Bentgården in Feragen. They were knitted with green and black handspun yarn, but had seven repeats around. I decided to reduce the repeats to six, and added longer single-color cuffs.

INSTRUCTIONS
Sizes: Women's (Men's)

MATERIALS
Yarn:
CYCA #1 (fingering) Symre from Telespinn (80% Norwegian mohair, 20% Norwegian lamb's wool, 330 yd/302 m / 100 g)
Yarn Amounts:
Red-Violet S277: 50 (100) g
Light Gray S010: 50 (100)
Needles: U.S. size 0 (1.5) / 2 (2.5) mm, set of 5 dpn
Gauge: 34 (31) sts = 4 in / 10 cm. Adjust needle size to obtain correct gauge if necessary.

RIGHT MITTEN
With Red-Violet, CO 77 sts. Divide sts over 4 dpn and join to work in the round. Work in "corrugated" cuff as follows:
Rnd 1: (P1, k10) around.
Rnd 2: *P1, k2tog, k2, yo, k2, yo, k2, k2tog tbl*; rep * to * around.
Rep Rnds 1-2 until cuff measures 4 (3¼) in / 10 (8) cm.
On the next rnd, dec evenly spaced around to 70 sts. Continue in charted pattern.

Increase for the thumb gusset as shown. At the dark line, set aside 13 sts for the thumb (see page 15 for details). Continue following the chart. Shape top as shown on chart. (see page 13 for details). Cut yarn and draw end through rem sts; tighten.

THUMB
Pick up and knit 15 + 15 sts = 30 sts total around thumbhole. Divide sts onto 4 dpn and work in pattern as shown on thumb chart. Cut yarn and draw end through rem sts; tighten.

LEFT MITTEN
Work mirror-image following the chart.

FINISHING
Weave in all ends neatly on WS. For a nice wavy edge to the cuff, pin out each point. Spray the mittens with water until thoroughly dampened and leave to dry for at least 24 hours.

The cuff on the men's version is folded double.

☐ Natural White—knit

☒ Natural White—purl

▨ Red—knit

FOOT

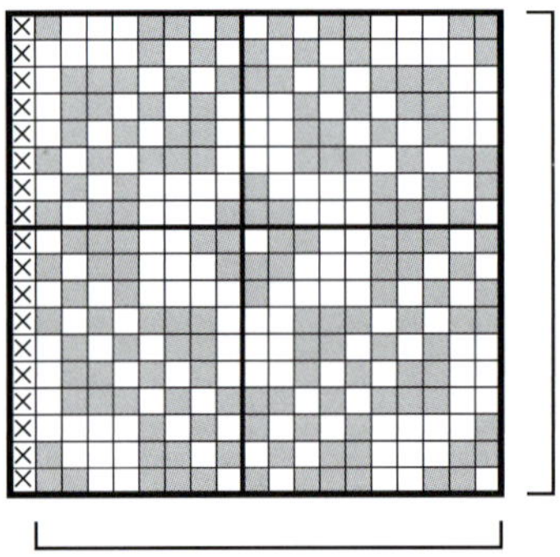

LEG

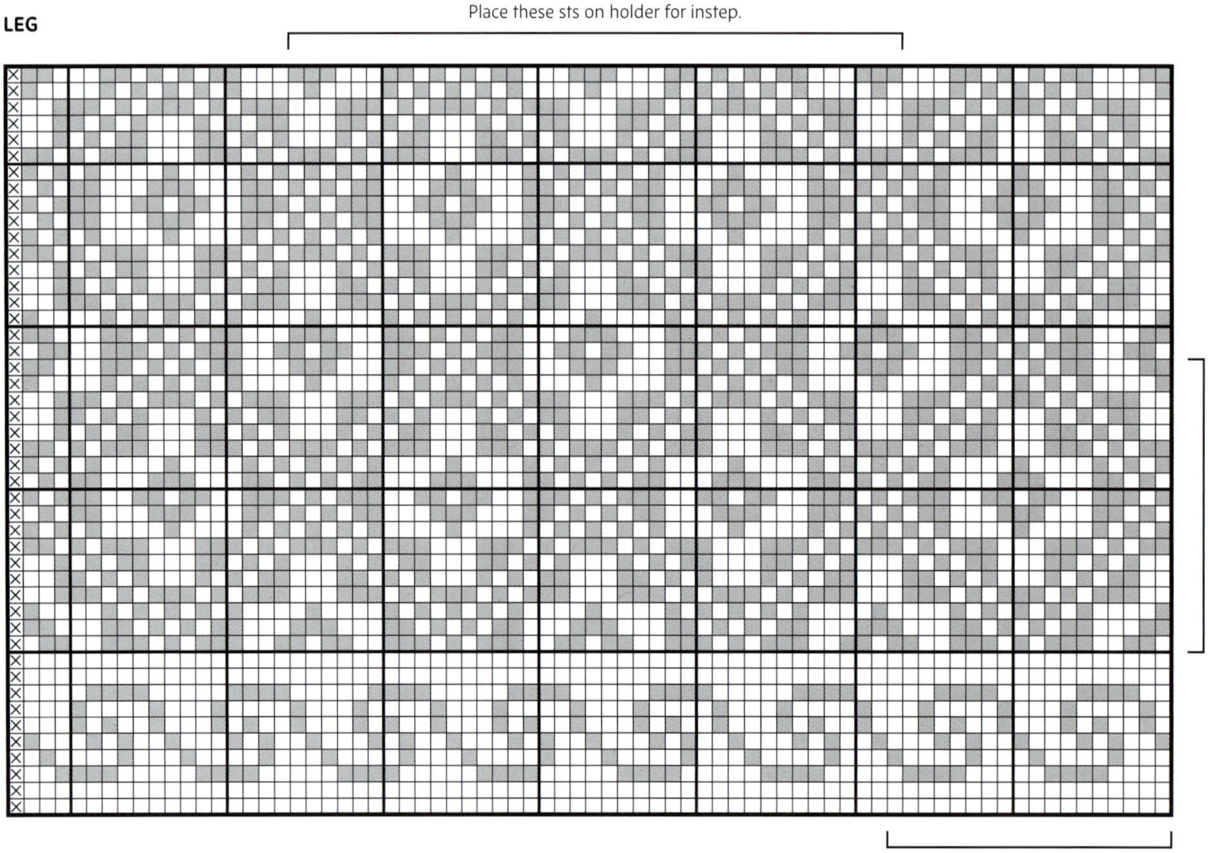

Trønder Socks

The Sverresborg Trøndelag Folk Museum has two pairs of stockings in fine red and white cotton yarn. The basic pattern for these stockings is the same, but they have slightly different finishing at the top. It's possible the same person knitted both pairs. The information that came with the stockings is sparse. About one pair, it says: "From Karen Aune's estate." These stockings have an extra rose panel at the top. The other pair is listed as: "Inherited from Mrs. Paulsen, née Brenne, who had received them from an old woman in Hegra." The Hegra stockings were the inspiration for these socks.

INSTRUCTIONS
Sizes: Women's (Men's)

MATERIALS
Yarn:
CYCA #1 (fingering) Mini Sterk from Du Store Alpakka (40% alpaca, 40% Merino wool, 20% polyamide, 182 yd/166 m / 50 g)
Yarn Colors and Amounts:
Natural White 806: 50 (50) g
Red 828: 50 (50) g
Needles: U. S. size 1.5 (2.5) / 2.5 (3) mm: set of 5 dpn
Gauge: 34 (32) sts in pattern = 4 in / 10 cm.
Adjust needle size to obtain correct gauge if necessary.

LEG
With Natural, CO 72 sts. Divide sts evenly onto 4 dpn. Join, being careful not to twist cast-on row; pm for beginning of rnd. Work around in k2, p2 ribbing for 8 rnds. Increasing 2 sts at center back on the first rnd, work following the leg chart. Always purl the center back stitch.

COMMON HEEL
After completing sock leg, divide the sts, placing 39 sts on a holder (see chart) for instep. These sts will "rest" until the heel is finished.

Heel Flap
Decrease 1 st at center back. Divide the remaining 34 stitches onto two dpn (Ndls A and B with 17 sts on each) and work back and forth with Natural. Begin with the RS facing you.
Row 1 (RS): Sl 1 purlwise wyb, knit rem sts on Ndls A and B.
Row 2: Sl 1 purlwise wyf, purl all rem sts on Ndls A and B.
Repeat these 2 rows until there are 13 chain sts at each side of the flap.

Shaping the Heel
Now you will shape the center back by decreasing as follows:
Row 1: Sl 1, knit until 5 sts rem on Ndl A, k2tog, k3. On Ndl B, k3, ssk, knit to end of needle.
Row 2: Sl 1, purl to end of row.
Row 3: Sl 1, knit until 4 sts rem on Ndl A, k2tog, k2. On Ndl B, k2, ssk, knit to end of needle.
Row 4: Sl 1, purl to end of row.
Row 5: Sl 1, knit until 3 sts rem on Ndl A, k2tog, k1. On Ndl B, k1, ssk, knit to end of needle.
Row 6: Sl 1, purl to end of row.
Row 7: Sl 1, knit until 2 sts rem on Ndl A, k2tog. On Ndl B, ssk, knit to end of needle.
Row 8: Sl 1, purl to end of Ndl B. Yarn is now at center of heel flap.
Hold the two dpn with RS facing in (so WS faces out on each side). Join the sets of sts with 3-needle BO: K2tog with 1 st from each needle, *k2tog with next st from each needle, pass first st over the second*. Repeat from * to * until 1 st loop rem.

FOOT
Divide the instep sts onto 2 dpn. With RS facing, Natural (carrying Red), and Ndl 1, beginning at the center of the sole, pick up and knit 1 st in each chain st on the side of the flap. You can pick up the chain sts through back loops or knit them tbl on the next rnd. Work the instep sts on Ndls 2-3, in pattern following the chart. With Ndl 4, pick up and knit sts on opposite side of heel flap = 74 sts total.
Work foot in pattern following the foot chart until length is 7-8 in / 18-20 cm or desired length before toe.

STAR TOE
With Natural, begin at the center of the sole. Knit 1 rnd before you begin toe shaping.
Rnd 1: (K5, k2tog) around. The 4 sts rem on Ndl 4 will be decreased in subsequent rnds.
Rnds 2-6: Knit.
Rnd 7: (K4, k2tog) around.
Rnds 8-11: Knit.
Rnd 12: (K3, k2tog) around.
Rnds 13-15: Knit
Rnd 16: (K2, k2tog) around.
Rnds 17-18: Knit.
Rnd 19: (K1, k2tog) around.
Rnd 20: Knit.
Rnd 21: (K2tog) around.

FINISHING
Cut yarn and draw end through rem sts; tighten. Weave in all ends neatly on WS. Make the second sock the same way.

□ White—knit
■ Black—knit
⊡ Inc 1 st with Black.

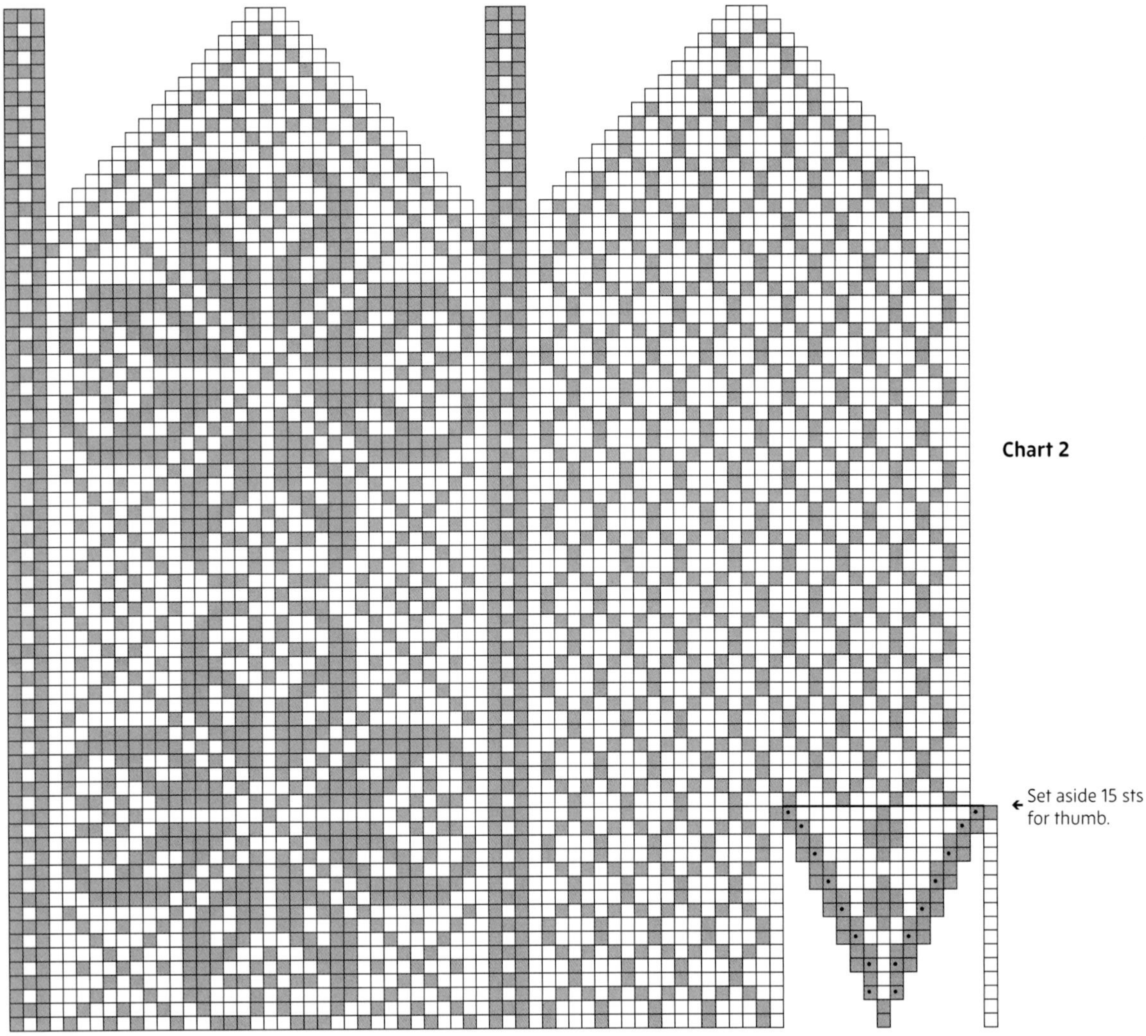

Chart 2

Chart 1

Thumb:

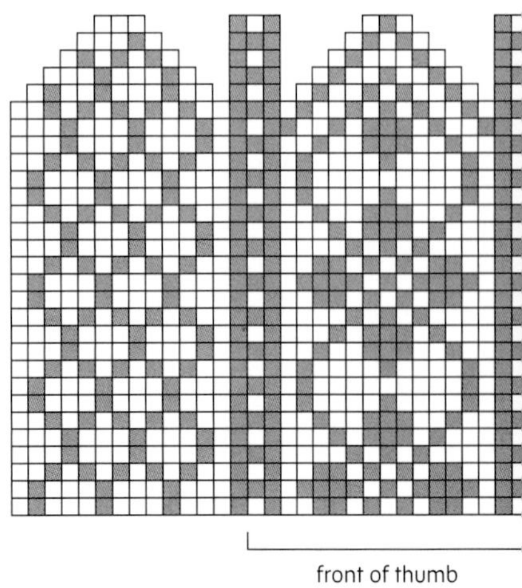

Selbu Mittens with "Six-Petaled Roses"

The typical Selbu mitten consists of a mitten "leaf" with a cuff (*vekk* is the local word)—which is to say, with a ribbing or decorative finish. The front and back sides of the mitten "leaf" had different motifs. In between was a vertical stripe. The thumb also had a front and back with different motifs, and a vertical stripe in between. Another characteristic of Selbu mittens is the marked difference between men's and women's mittens—something very few of us reflect on today. Traditionally, women's mittens had ribbed cuffs, while men's mittens had patterns on the cuffs.

INSTRUCTIONS
Sizes: Women's (Men's)

MATERIALS
Yarn:
CYCA #1 (fingering) Gammelserie from Rauma (100% wool, 175 yd/160 m / 50 g)
Yarn Amounts
Black 436: 50 (100) g
White 400: 50 (100) g
Needles: U.S. size 000 (0) / 1.5 (2) mm, set of 5 dpn
Gauge: 35 (32) sts = 4 in / 10 cm. Adjust needle size to obtain correct gauge if necessary.

Version 1
Striped Ribbing
With Black, CO 60 sts. Divide sts over 4 dpn and join to work in the round. Work 4 rnds k2, p2 ribbing. Continue in ribbing, alternating 2 rnds White and 2 rnds Black until there are a total of 6 White stripes. End with 4 rnds Black.

Version 2
Patterned Cuff
With White, CO 60 sts. Divide sts over 4 dpn and join to work in the round. Work 4 rnds k1, p1 ribbing. Continue in St st, following Chart 1.

RIGHT MITTEN
When the cuff is complete, continue on to Chart 2. Increase for the thumb gusset as shown. At the dark line, place 15 sts on a holder for the thumb. CO 14 sts over the gap and continue following the chart. Shape top as shown on chart (see page 13 for details). Cut yarn and draw end through rem sts; tighten.

THUMB
Pick up and knit 17 + 15 sts = 32 sts total around thumbhole. Divide sts onto 4 dpn and work as shown on thumb chart. Cut yarn and draw end through rem sts; tighten.

LEFT MITTEN
Work mirror-image following the chart.

FINISHING
Weave in all ends neatly on WS. Gently steam press under a damp pressing cloth to block.

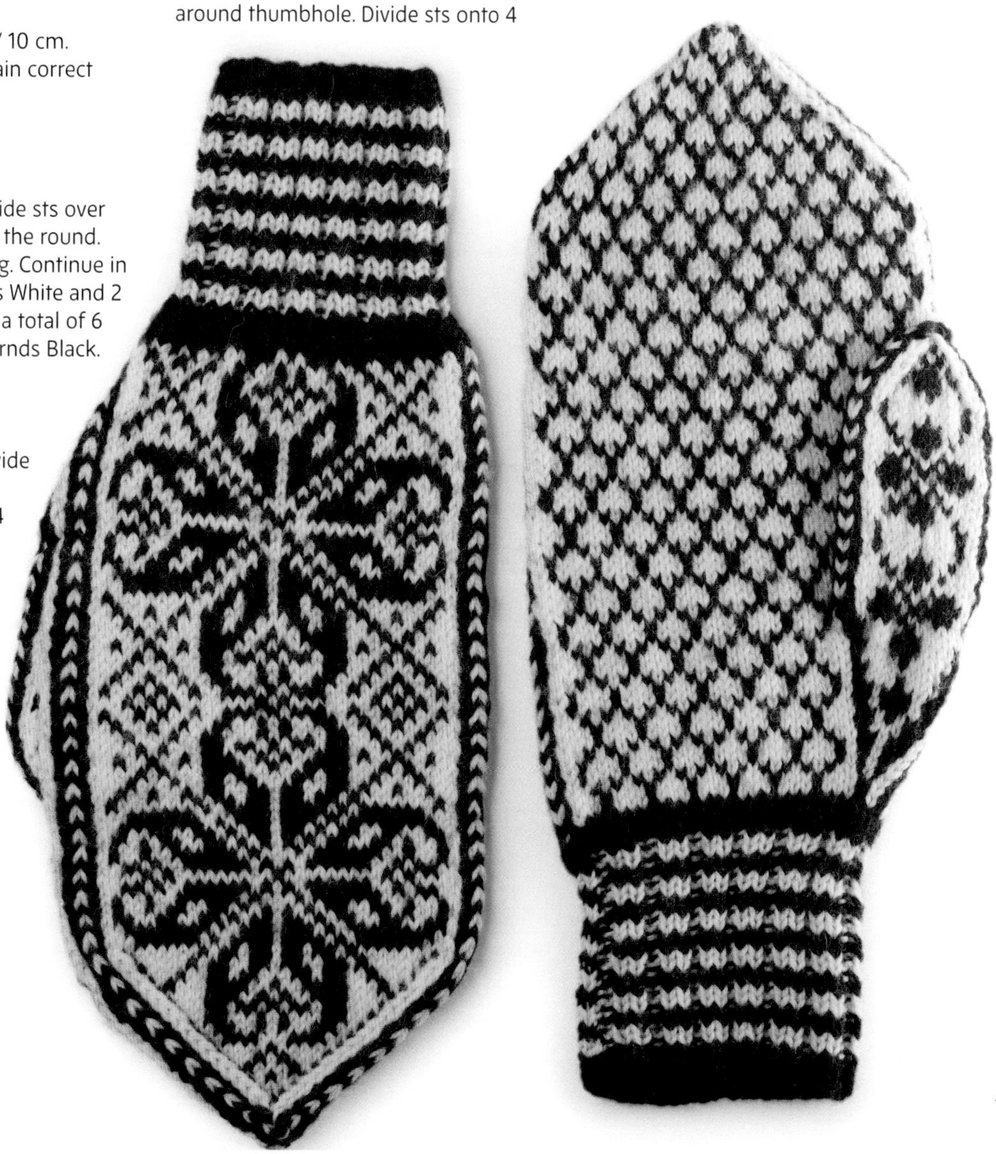

- □ White—knit
- ▩ Black—knit
- ⊡ CO 1 st with White
- ▣ CO 1 st with Black

CHART 3: THUMB

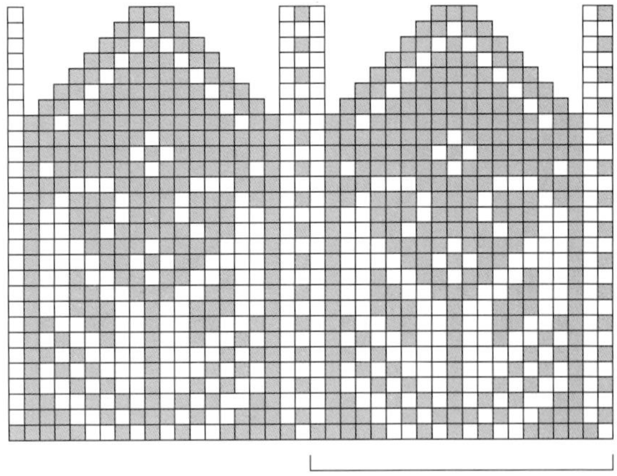

front of thumb

CHART 2

Set aside 19 sts for thumb.

CHART 1

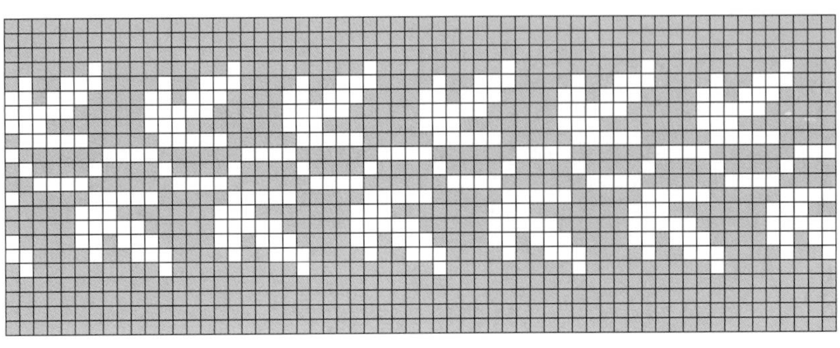

Rose Mittens from Selbu

Classic Selbu mittens were made differently for women and men. As a general rule, women's mittens began with a ribbed cuff, and later on, a lace-patterned cuff. These were often decorated with simple stripes, too. Men's mittens, by contrast, always had a decorative colorwork cuff—so this design is technically for a pair of men's mittens. If you want to hold to tradition and knit these as women's mittens, you can substitute ribbing for the leaf panel.

INSTRUCTIONS
Sizes: Women's (Men's)

MATERIALS
Yarn:
CYCA #1 (fingering) Gammelserie from Rauma (100% wool, 175 yd/160 m / 50 g:
Black 436: 100 (100) g
White 401: 50 (100) g
Needles: U.S. size 0 (1.5) / 2 (2.5) mm, set of 5 dpn
Gauge: 34 (31) sts = 4 in / 10 cm. Adjust needle size to obtain correct gauge if necessary.

RIGHT MITTEN
With Black, CO 60 sts. Divide sts over 4 dpn and join to work in the round. Knit 4 rnds.
Eyelet Rnd: *K2tog, yo*; rep * to * around.
Work following Chart 1. On last rnd, increase to 61 sts. Continue, following Chart 2. Increase as shown, and at dark line, place 19 sts on holder for thumb. Shape top as shown on chart.

THUMB
Pick up and knit 20 + 20 sts = 40 sts total around thumbhole. Divide sts onto 4 dpn and work in pattern as shown on Chart 3 for thumb. Make sure the patterns align. After completing chart rows, cut yarn and draw end through rem sts; tighten.

LEFT MITTEN
Work mirror-image following the chart.

FINISHING
Fold in cuff at foldline (eyelet rnd) and sew down edge on WS. Weave in all ends neatly on WS. Gently steam press under a damp pressing cloth to block.

LIEBESKIND
Berlin

Thumb:

□ Gray—knit
■ Blue—knit

The Folk Museum's Selbu Mittens

The Norwegian Folk Museum in Oslo has several Selbu mittens. About the pair used as the basis for this design, it says "Brukssted: Selbu." It also states that the mittens were transferred from the Art Industry Museum in 1955. The pattern is not typical for Selbu. On the other hand, the original pair could have been knitted before it was usual to knit for sale.

INSTRUCTIONS
Sizes: Women's (Men's)

MATERIALS
Yarn:
CYCA #1 (fingering) Babyull from Dale (100% Merino wool, 180 yd/165 m / 50 g), Blue 5545: 50 (100) g
CYCA #1 (fingering) Lanett Babyull Superwash from Sandnes Garn (100% Merino Wool, 191 yd/175 m / 50 g), Gray 1032: 50 (100) g
Needles: U.S. size 0 (1.5) / 2 (2.5) mm, set of 5 dpn
Gauge: 37 (34) sts = 4 in / 10 cm. Adjust needle size to obtain correct gauge if necessary.

RIGHT MITTEN
With Blue, CO 80 sts. Divide sts over 4 dpn and join to work in the round. Work in St st for ⅜ in / 1 cm. Purl 1 rnd for foldline and then continue, following the chart.
Increase for the thumb gusset as shown. At the dark line, set aside 15 sts for the thumb (see page 15 for details). Continue following the chart. Shape top as shown on chart. Cut yarn and draw end through rem sts; tighten.

THUMB
Pick up and knit 17 + 17 sts = 34 sts total around thumbhole. Divide sts onto 4 dpn and work in pattern as shown on thumb chart. Cut yarn and draw end through rem sts; tighten.

LEFT MITTEN
Work mirror-image following the chart.

FINISHING
Weave in all ends neatly on WS. Fold the cuff under at the foldline and loosely sew down edge on WS. Gently steam press under a damp pressing cloth to block.

Mittens from Lierne

The Sverresborg Trøndelag Folk Museum was given a pair of mittens, knitted with black and white wool, from someone who received them in 1919. The mittens originally had the same pattern all around, but the inside of the palm seems to have gotten so worn that it was re-knitted with a different yarn and pattern. I've reconstructed the original patterning.

INSTRUCTIONS
Sizes: Women's (Men's)

MATERIALS
Yarn:
CYCA #1 (fingering) Gammelserie from Rauma (100% wool, 175 yd/160 m / 50 g), Red 424: 50 (100) g
CYCA #1 (fingering) Babyull from Dale (100% Merino wool, 180 yd/165 m / 50 g), Pink 4516: 50 (100) g
Needles: U.S. sizes 0 and 1.5 (1.5 and 2.5) / 2 and 2.5 (2.5 and 3) mm, set of 5 dpn
Gauge: 28 (25) sts = 4 in / 10 cm. Adjust needle sizes to obtain correct gauge if necessary.

RIGHT MITTEN
With Red and smaller needles, CO 72 sts. Divide sts over 4 dpn and join to work in the round. Work around in k2, p1 ribbing for 2¾ in (7 cm). Change to larger dpn and St st. Continue, following the chart. At the dark line, set aside 12 sts for the thumb (see page 15 for details). Continue, following the chart. Shape top as shown (see page 13 for details). Cut yarn and draw end through rem sts; tighten.

THUMB
Pick up and knit 14 + 14 sts = 28 sts total around thumbhole. Divide sts onto 4 dpn and work in pattern as shown on thumb chart. Cut yarn and draw end through rem sts; tighten.

LEFT MITTEN
Work mirror-image following the chart.

FINISHING
Weave in all ends neatly on WS. Gently steam press under a damp pressing cloth to block.

Thumb:

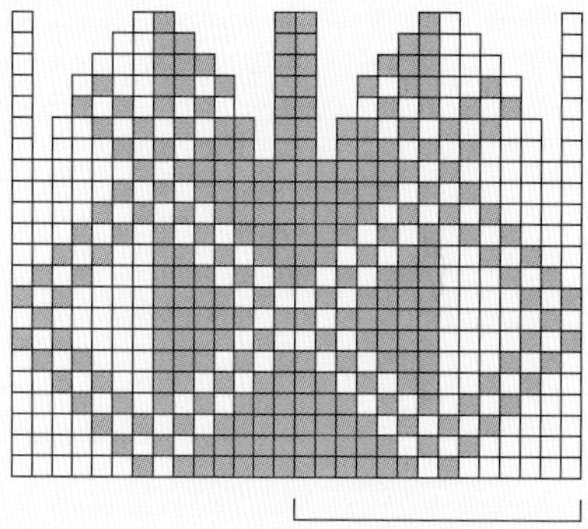
front

■ Red—knit
□ Pink—knit

← Set aside 12 sts for thumb.

CHART 2: FOOT

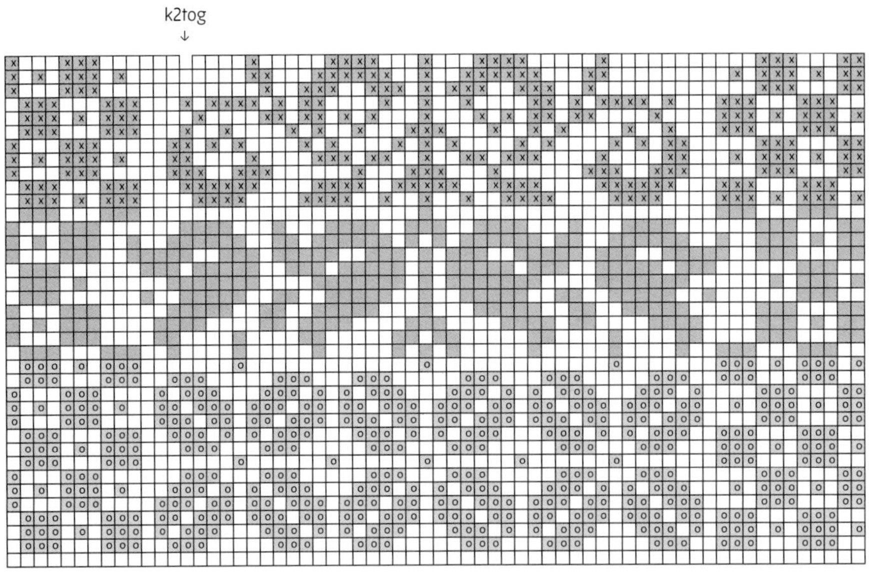

CHART 1: LEG

- Color 1—knit
- Color 1—purl
- Color 2 (MC)—knit
- Color 2 (MC)—purl
- Color 3—knit
- Color 4—knit
- Color 4—purl

Spring In Your Step Socks

Dress your feet in spring's colors and flowers! These cozy socks are perfect for early spring days when the weather's still a little chilly.

INSTRUCTIONS

Sizes: Women's S (Women's L)
Leg Circumference: Approx. 9½ (10¼) in / 24 (26) cm.
Leg Length: Approx. 8 in / 20 cm when finished.
If you want a slightly wider leg, knit a bit more loosely. If you want a narrower leg, knit a bit more tightly. Remember, though, wool is quite elastic.

MATERIALS

Yarn:
CYCA #1 (fingering) Mini Sterk from Du Store Alpakka (40% alpaca, 40% Merino wool, 20% polyamide, 182 yd/166 m / 50 g)
Yarn Colors and Amounts:
Color 1: Burnt Orange 842: 50 (50) g
Color 2 (MC): Light Rose Pink 850: 100 (100) g
Color 3: Yellow-Green 843: 50 (50) g
Color 4: Golden Yellow 835: 50 (50) g
Needles: U. S. size 1.5 (2.5) / 2.5 (3) mm: set of 5 dpn
Gauge: 28 (26) sts in pattern = 4 in / 10 cm.
Adjust needle size to obtain correct gauge if necessary.

LEG

With Color 1, CO 68 sts. Divide sts evenly over 4 dpn. Join, being careful not to twist cast-on row; pm for beginning of rnd. Work around in (k2, p2) ribbing as shown on Chart 1, for 4 rnds. Continue in stockinette and pattern, following chart. Always purl the center back st. After completing first flower panel, decrease 1 st at each side of the center back purl st = 66 sts rem. K2tog on left side of purl st. Knit to end of rnd, and on right side of purl st, k2tog tbl.

Continue in stockinette and pattern with the purl st at center back. After 10 rnds, decrease 2 more sts as before and as shown on chart = 64 sts rem.

HOURGLASS HEEL

After completing charted rows for leg, 64 sts rem. Divide sts, placing the 32 sts for the instep on a holder. These sts will "rest" until the heel is finished.

Arrange rem 32 sts at center back (see chart) on one dpn. Hold the sock so the back side with the purl st faces you, and begin working back and forth on right side with color 4.

Row 1: Knit across; turn.
Row 2: Begin row with yo, sl 1 (yo + sl 1 = DS), purl to end of row; turn.
Row 3: Yo, sl 1 knit to DS; turn.
Row 4: Yo, sl 1, purl to DS; turn.
Rep Rows 3-4 until there are 11 DS on each side and 10 single sts in the middle. Knit all around the sock (including instep sts on hold) 2 times. Join each DS (yo + slipped st) as 1 st.
Place the 32 instep sts on hold again while you complete the heel.
Row 1: Knit the 10 sts at center of heel + k1; turn.
Row 2: Yo, sl 1, purl the 10 sts at center + p1; turn.
Row 3: Yo, sl 1, knit the single sts and knit each DS as one st + k1; turn.
Row 4: Yo, sl 1, purl to DS, purl DS as one st + p1; turn.
Rep Rows 3-4 until 32 single sts rem on sole; heel is now complete.

FOOT

Count your sts; there should be 64 sts total before you knit around following Chart 2. The rnd begins at the center of sole.

NOTE: Decrease 1 st on last rnd with k2tog = 63 sts rem (see arrow on top of Chart 2).

Try on sock to see if foot length matches your foot length before toe. If the sock is a bit short, knit a few extra rnds with the next color (Color 1) before you begin toe shaping.

STAR TOE

Shape toe as follows (the numbers outside the parentheses are for the small size and the numbers inside parentheses are for size large).
Change to Color 1 and work as follows:
Decrease Rnd 1: *K5, k2tog*; rep * to * around. Knit 5 (6) rnds.
Decrease Rnd 2: *K4, k2tog*; rep * to * around. Knit 4 (5) rnds
Decrease Rnd 3: *K3, k2tog*; rep * to * around. Knit 3 (4) rnds
Decrease Rnd 4: *K2, k2tog*; rep * to * around. Knit 2 (3) rnds
Decrease Rnd 5: *K1, k2tog*; rep * to * around. Knit 1 (2) rnds
Decrease Rnd 6: *K2tog*; rep * to * around.

FINISHING

Cut yarn and draw end through rem sts; tighten. Weave in all ends neatly on WS. Make the second sock the same way.

Thumb:

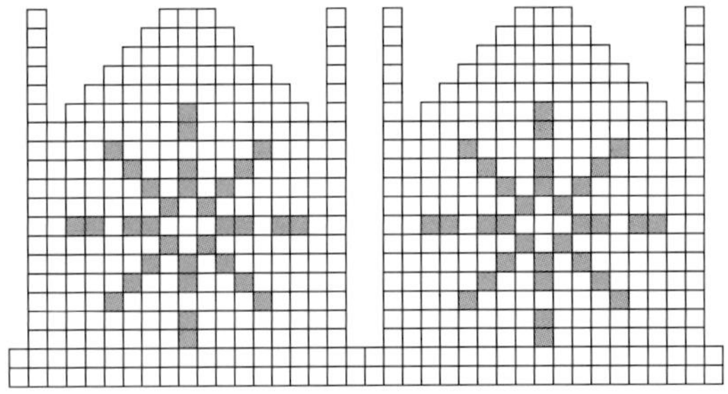

□ White—knit
■ Blue—knit
▣ Blue—purl

Set aside 17 sts for thumb.

Snowflake Mittens

All sorts of stars have been widely used as motifs in Norwegian knitted textiles. The stars featured on the palms of these mittens are often knitted in Selbu and are locally called "spit balls." Many Norwegian designers have used snowflakes in their designs and I wanted to make my own snowflakes.

INSTRUCTIONS
Sizes: Women's (Men's)

MATERIALS
Yarn:
CYCA #1 (fingering) Dale Baby Ull (100% wool, 180 yd/165 m / 50 g), White 0017: 50 (100) g
CYCA #2 (sport) Arroyo from Malabrigo (100% Merino wool, 335 yd/306 m / 100 g), Azules 856: 50 (100) g OR substitute Dale Baby Ull, Blue 5545
Needles: U.S. size 1.5 (2.5) / 2.5 (3) mm, set of 5 dpn
Gauge: 32 (29) sts = 4 in / 10 cm. Adjust needle size to obtain correct gauge if necessary.

RIGHT MITTEN
With Blue, CO 62 sts. Divide sts onto 4 dpn and join, being careful not to twist cast-on row. Work around in k1, p1 ribbing for the first rnd, as shown on the chart. Purl the next rnd. Now continue in St st following the chart. Increase for the thumb gusset as indicated on the chart until there are 17 sts for the thumb. Place the 17 sts on a holder and CO 16 sts over the gap. Continue the pattern and shape the top as shown on the chart (see page 13 for details). Cut yarn and draw end through rem sts; tighten.

THUMB
Pick up 19 + 19 sts around the thumbhole = 38 sts total. Divide sts onto 4 dpn and work as shown on thumb chart. Cut yarn and draw end through rem sts; tighten.

LEFT MITTEN
Work mirror-image from chart.

FINISHING
Weave in all ends neatly on WS. Gently steam press under a damp pressing cloth to block.

Spider Socks from Troms

A rather common pattern element we find in several places around Norway is called *skarttrell* or *kongoro* in Selbu. *Kongro* is an old Norse name for a spider or daddy longlegs. One pair of women's stockings from Troms, registered by The Norwegian Institute for Bunad and Folk Costume, features *kongro* patterns in a tight block net—a type of spider web, if you will. The stockings were knitted with heathery light and dark gray wool yarns. Here, the *kongro* pattern is structured to repeat as an endless pattern. An endless pattern is one which has no beginning or end. It continues for all eternity.

INSTRUCTIONS
Sizes: Women's (Men's)

MATERIALS
Yarn:
CYCA #1 (fingering) 2-ply lamb's Rya wool from Lykkesau (100% organic lamb's wool, 284 yd/260 m / 100 g)
Or, substitute:
CYCA #1 (fingering) 2-ply Gammelserie from Rauma (100% wool, 175 yd/160 m / 50 g)
Yarn Colors and Amounts:
Natural Dark Gray: 100 (100) g
Natural Light Gray: 100 (100) g
Needles: U. S. size 2.5 (4) / 3 (3.5) mm: set of 5 dpn
Gauge: 30 (28) sts in pattern = 4 in / 10 cm.
Adjust needle size to obtain correct gauge if necessary.

LEG
With Dark Gray, CO 62 sts. Divide sts as evenly as possible onto 4 dpn. Join, being careful not to twist cast-on row; pm for beginning of rnd. Work around in (k1tbl, p1) ribbing for 1½ in / 4 cm. Knit 1 rnd, increasing 1 st at center back = 63 sts. Continue, following chart.

HOURGLASS HEEL
After completing charted rows for leg, divide the sts, placing 35 sts for the instep on a holder. These sts will "rest" until the heel is finished.

Arrange rem 28 sts at center back (see chart) on one dpn and work back and forth with Dark Gray.

Row 1 (RS): Knit across; turn.
Row 2: Sl 1 purlwise wyf, purl until 1 st rem; turn.
Row 3: Sl 1, knit until 1 st rem; turn.
Row 4: Sl 1, purl until 2 sts rem; turn.
Row 5: Sl 1, knit until 2 sts rem; turn.
Continue the same way with 1 less st before each turn until 10 sts rem at the center of the heel. The last row is on RS.
Sl 1, purl as many sts as were last knitted. Pick up the strand between the last and next st, twist it and purl it tog with the next st; turn.
Sl 1, knit as many sts as last worked. Pick up the strand between the last st and the next, twist it and knit it together with the next st; turn.
Continue, repeating these 2 rows.
You should have 1 more st each time before you turn.

NOTE: Tighten the yarn a bit each time you turn to avoid holes.
Continue with 1 more st on each row until you work across all the sts on the last row.

Now work around on all sts following chart, a total of 32 rnds. Make sure the pattern on the foot matches the leg pattern. If necessary, add or subtract rounds to lengthen or shorten foot.

STAR TOE
Begin at the center of the sole.
Rnd 1: (K5, k2tog) around.
Rnds 2-6: Knit.
Rnd 7: (K4, k2tog) around.
Rnds 8-11: Knit.
Rnd 12: (K3, k2tog) around.
Rnds 13-15: Knit
Rnd 16: (K2, k2tog) around.
Rnds 17-18: Knit.
Rnd 19: (K1, k2tog) around.
Rnd 20: Knit.
Rnd 21: (K2tog) around.

FINISHING
Cut yarn and draw end through rem sts; tighten. Weave in all ends neatly on WS. Make the second sock the same way.

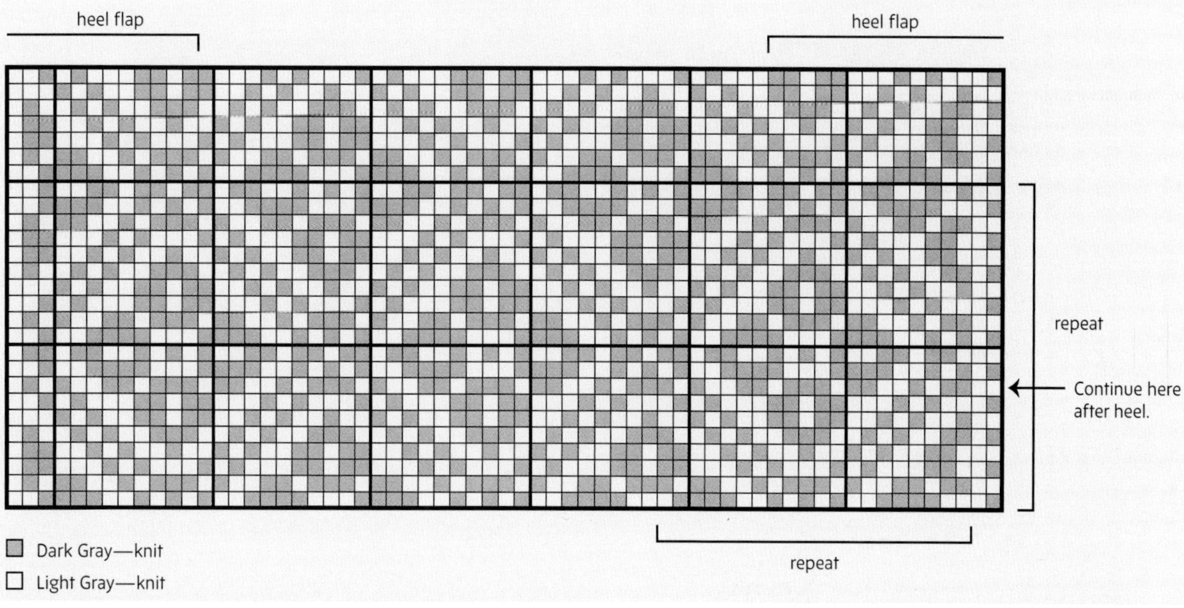

Thumb:

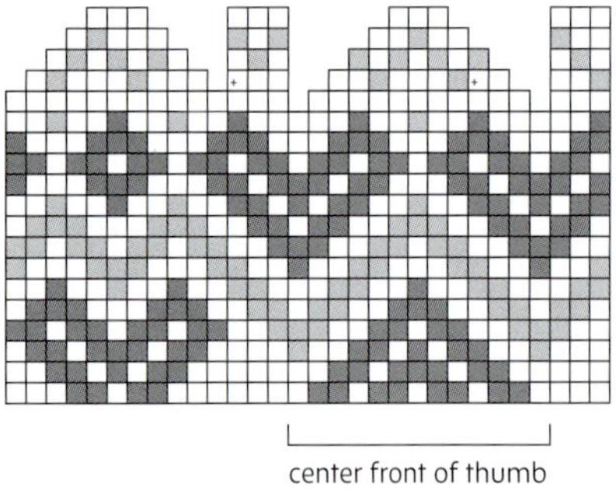

Braided cord:

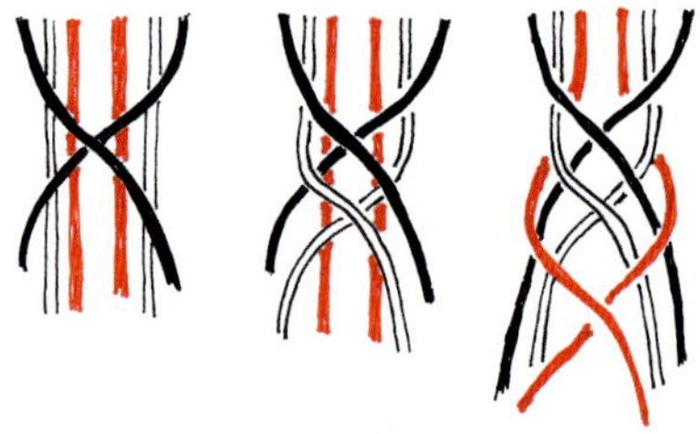

☐ White—knit

■ Red—knit

▨ Blue—knit

Mittens from Kautokeino

Berit Hætta writes that after sheep holding began, spinning, weaving, and knitting were common amongst the settled Sami. "In Kautokeino, the knitted mitten has had a very interesting development from the end of the 19th century up until now. After they learned how to dye yarn or could buy yarn in many colors, the mittens were knitted with colorful, self-designed patterns which embellished the entire mitten." The background color was preferably white, with red, blue, and green as common pattern colors. These mittens were made to look like a pair sold at Husfliden (a handcrafts shop) in Kautokeino in the 1950s.

INSTRUCTIONS
Sizes: Women's (Men's)

MATERIALS
Yarn:
CYCA #2 (sport) PT2 from Rauma (100% wool, 180 yd/165 m / 50 g)
Yarn Amounts:
Red 88: 50 (100 g)
Blue 36: 50 (100) g
White 00: 50 (100) g
Needles: U.S. size 1.5 (2.5) / 2.5 (3) mm: straights and set of 5 dpn
Gauge: 29 (26) sts = 4 in / 10 cm. Adjust needle size to obtain correct gauge if necessary.

RIGHT MITTEN
With Red around thumb and White over index finger, use long-tail method to CO 72 sts. Divide sts evenly over 4 dpn and join to work in the round. Work 1 rnd two-end purl braid (see page 14) with Red and White. Work another rnd of purl braid with Red and Blue.

Continue, following the chart. At the dark line, set aside 13 sts for the thumb (see page 15 for details). Shape top as shown (see page 13 for details). Cut yarn and draw end through rem sts; tighten.

THUMB
Pick up and knit 15 + 15 sts = 30 sts total around thumbhole. Divide sts onto 4 dpn and work following the thumb chart. Cut yarn and draw end through rem sts; tighten.

LEFT MITTEN
Work mirror-image following the chart.

FINISHING
Weave in all ends neatly on WS. Gently steam press under a damp pressing cloth to block.

BRAIDED CORDS
Measure two strands of each color, about 35½ in / 90 cm long each. Thread through edge of mitten, opposite thumb, so strands are doubled = 12 strands each about 17¾ / 45 cm long. Group the strands so you have 2 Red, 2 White, and 2 Blue. Braid as shown in the drawing on page 178.

TASSELS
Wind the yarn 7-8 times around four fingers held together or until tassel is thick enough. Cut a strand to wrap 2-3 times around near the top of the tassel and fasten off securely (the end can be slid under the wraps and down into the tassel. Cut bottom loops open; attach tassel to cord.

Bibliography

Andresen, Tine: *Strikkebok til Skole- og huusbrug*. Boghandler J.Bagners Forlag, Helsingør 1847.

Bjelland, Anna Marøy, Dietrichson, Dagny og Egge, Ågot: *Votter og vanter*. Aschehoug 1955.

Blom, Marie: *Husraad og Opskrifter til Veiledning for hvermand*. P.T. Mallings Boghandels Forlag, Kristiania 1888.

Engelstad, Helen (red): *Forming i 100 år. Fra Den kvindelige Industriskole i Christiania til Statens lærerskole i forming Oslo*. Oslo 1975.

Fossnes, Heidi: *Håndplagg til bunader og folkedrakter*. N.W. Damm & Søn 2003.

Gravjord, Ingebjørg: *Votten i norsk tradisjon*. Landbruksforlaget 1986.

Halvorsen, Caroline: *Strikkebog for barneskolen og hjemmet*. J.W. Cappelens forlag, Kristiania 1901.

Haugen, Anny: *Samisk husflid i Finnmark*. Landbruksforlaget 1987.

Heggtveit, Thor Arne: Slektsdatabase. heggtveit.no.

Jensen, Inger: «Kvinnehår i fiskervott.». Norsk Husflid nr. 2 1988.

Kjellberg, Anne, Gravjord, Ingebjørg, Rosander, Gerd Aarsland og Svendsen, Anne-Lise: *Strikking i Norge*. Norges Husflidslag / Landbruksforlaget 1987.

Koch, Hanna-Kirsti og Hals, Aagot M: *Alle kvinners strikkebok*. Oslo 1940.

Lerche, Adéle (red): *Gyldendal Store Sy- & Håndarbeidsbok*. Gyldendal norsk forlag 1963.

Lønnå, Elisabeth: Caroline Halvorsen. «Norsk biografisk leksikon.». Snl.no.

Noss Aagot: *Med ein fot i mellomalderen. Vadmål sokkar og annan slag fotbunad i Tinn i Telemark*. By og Bygd. Norsk Folkemuseums årbok 1987–88. Bind XXXII.

Næss, Hans Eyvind: *Trolldomsprosessene i Norge på 1600-tallet: En retts- og sosialhistorisk undersøkelse*. Universitetsforlaget, Oslo 1982.

Reitan, Janne: «Selbustrikking – kompetanse for morgendagen.». HIO 1992.

Reitan, Janne: «Improvisation in Tradition.». Doktorgradsavhandling ved HIO 2005.

Rutt, Richard: *A History of Hand Knitting*. Batsford, 1987. Interweave, 1987.

Trætteberg, Gunvor Ingstad: *Skinnhyre og sjøklær. Fiskerbondens utrustning på 1700- og 1800-tallet*. Landbruksforlaget 1999.

En ny attåtnæring: Selbustrikkinga. selbuboka.no.

Sibbern, Annichen: *Norske strikkemønstre*. Grøndahl & Søn's forlag, Oslo 1928. Norwegian Knitting Designs. Grondahl & Son, 1965.

Sundbø, Annemor: *Kvardagsstrikk. Kulturskattar frå fillehaugen*. Det norske samlaget 1994. *Everyday Knitting: Treasures from a Ragpile*. Torridal Tweed, 2000.

Sæther, Nina Granlund: *Hjertet i folkekunsten – en hyllest til håndens arbeid*. N.W. Damm & Søn 2001.

Sæther, Nina Granlund: *Votter. Strikkemønstre fra hele Norge*. Cappelen Damm 2015.
Mittens from Around Norway. Trafalgar Square Books, 2017.

Sæther, Nina Granlund: *Sokker fra hele Norge*.
Cappelen Damm 2017. *Socks from Around Norway*. Trafalgar Square Books, 2019.

Ugelstad: Janike Sverdrup: «Ola Hansson i nytt lys.» By og bygd nr. 44. Norsk Folkemuseum 2011.

Folketelling 1801 for 1640P Røros prestegjeld. Digitalarkivet. arkivverket.no.

Yarn Information

Anzula yarns are available from stores listed by:
Anzula
anzula.com

Blacker yarns are available from:
The Woolly Thistle
thewoollythistle.com

Malabrigo yarns are available from stores listed by:
Malabrigo
malabrigoyarn.com

Hedgehog Fibres yarns are available (with international shipping charges) from:
Hedgehog Fibres
shop.hedgehogfibres.com

Rauma yarns are available from:
The Yarn Guys
theyarnguys.com

The Woolly Thistle
thewoollythistle.com

Sandnes yarns may be purchased (with international shipping charges) from:
Scandinavian Knitting Design
scandinavianknittingdesign.com

Wool2dye4 undyed yarns are available from:
wool2dye4
wool2dye4.com

Some yarns—Dale, Du Store Alpakka, Filcolana, Hillesvåg Ullvarefabrikk, Hoelfeldt Lund, Lofoten Wool, Lykkesau, Mohair by Canard, Setesdal Handcraft, and Telespinn yarns in particular—may be difficult to find. A variety of additional and substitute yarns are available from:
Webs—America's Yarn Store
75 Service Center Road
Northampton, MA 01060
800-367-9327
yarn.com

LoveKnitting.com
loveknitting.com/us

If you are unable to obtain any of the yarn used in this book, it can be replaced with a yarn of a similar weight and composition. Please note, however, the finished projects may vary slightly from those shown, depending on the yarn used. Try www.yarnsub.com for suggestions.

For more information on selecting or substituting yarn, contact your local yarn shop or an online store; they are familiar with all types of yarns and would be happy to help you. Additionally, the online knitting community at Ravelry.com has forums where you can post questions about specific yarns. Yarns come and go so quickly these days and there are so many beautiful yarns available.